Speak Up Speak Out: Simple Success Strategies for the Speaking Business

Canadian Association of Professional Speakers, Vancouver Chapter

Printed in Victoria, Canada

Cover design by BG Communications, Vancouver, BC
Editing/book production by GF Murray Creative Information Solutions, Coquitlam, BC

All photographs reprinted by permission.

National Library of Canada Cataloguing in Publication

   Speak up, speak out : simple success strategies for the speaking business / Canadian Association of Professional Speakers B.C.
ISBN 1-4120-0927-8
   1. Public speaking—Vocational guidance. I. Canadian Association of Professional Speakers. BC Chapter .
PN4098.S64 2003   808.5'1'023   C2003-904596-X

TRAFFORD

This book was published *on-demand* in cooperation with Trafford Publishing. On-demand publishing is a unique process and service of making a book available for retail sale to the public taking advantage of on-demand manufacturing and Internet marketing. **On-demand publishing** includes promotions, retail sales, manufacturing, order fulfilment, accounting and collecting royalties on behalf of the author.

Suite 6E, 2333 Government St., Victoria, B.C. V8T 4P4, CANADA

Phone	250-383-6864	Toll-free	1-888-232-4444 (Canada & US)
Fax	250-383-6804	E-mail	sales@trafford.com
Web site	www.trafford.com	TRAFFORD PUBLISHING IS A DIVISION OF TRAFFORD HOLDINGS LTD.
Trafford Catalogue #03-1296		www.trafford.com/robots/03-1296.html

10 9 8 7 6 5 4 3 2 1

Contents

A Message

This book is dedicated to you, the reader. The many authors who have contributed to the chapters have shared some of their greatest insights to developing and growing a business in the speaking, training and facilitating profession.

Our greatest wish is that this book will help you build on your vision and your gift of the spoken word so that they can be shared with many. It's also our way of introducing you to a group of professionals who willingly support each other by sharing their expertise. We invite you to use the information in this book as a guide and ongoing reference to developing your business.

Enjoy the journey!

Lynn Robinson and Elaine Allison
Co-chairs, CAPS Vancouver book project

President's Message

The speaking business is exciting, invigorating and challenging. Aside from the obvious challenges of speaking itself, as entrepreneurs we can also be challenged. It can be difficult to know what the best uses of our time are, or where to spend our money to best leverage our business and take it to the next level.

It can be a lonely business, too. We often work from home offices with no staff or maybe only a part-time employee, and our families and friends may not completely understand what it is we actually do for a living.

I was a classic lone-wolf entrepreneur when I started in my speaking practice in 1996—until I found out about CAPS in 1998. Since becoming a member, and especially since I began serving on the board, I have found that the people of CAPS have much wisdom, camaraderie and friendship to offer. I find myself wondering what I was doing in the years before I joined CAPS, when I was struggling to figure everything out on my own.

CAPS and its members can save you time by providing you with the answers needed to build your business. Ultimately they can help you make more money. If your membership results in just one speaking engagement from the web site listings or a referral from a colleague you will have multiplied your membership investment by at least threefold, depending on your fee level. There are many more tangible benefits to being a member, which you can find at **www.canadianspeakers.org**. Personally I find it is the affiliation with a group of professionals who have become friends that has been invaluable to me.

This book is a small slice of the best wisdom that the expert speakers of the CAPS Vancouver Chapter can offer. Enjoy!

Cheryl Cran
President, CAPS Vancouver 2003
CSP Candidate

About CAPS

The Canadian Association of Professional Speakers (CAPS) is "the association for experts who speak professionally" and for others who work with and support the speaking business. Our members represent all aspects of the speaking business, including keynoters, trainers and facilitators.

We help our members succeed with learning opportunities, networking, market development and professional accreditation. As a founding member of the International Federation for Professional Speakers (IFPS), CAPS has also shown leadership in advancing the speaking business worldwide.

Our membership categories (Professional, Associate and Candidate) are based on different levels of income and experience. The Certified Speaking Professional (CSP) designation is the only earned designation in the speaking profession and, as of 2003, is held by only twenty Canadians. Members of the Canadian Speaking Hall of Fame (HoF) are recognized for excellence on the platform, business success and contributions to the speaking industry. Affiliate membership is open to meeting planners, bureaus, salaried speakers, suppliers and people from other industry-related groups. All of our members must abide by our Code of Professional Ethics.

Our highly rated annual national convention is our flagship learning and community building opportunity. Make it a point to attend the upcoming convention, to be held in Toronto, Ontario, from December 4 to 6, 2003. Check out our web site to get more details at **www.canadianspeakers.org** .

CAPS has eleven chapters across Canada, from BC to Nova Scotia. Our chapters provide exceptional programming, educational and networking opportunities for speakers at all levels. Visitors are welcome. Thanks to our Professional level members from the Vancouver Chapter for their contributions to this value-packed publication. I know you will find something both personally and professionally within these pages.

Visit our new web site, located at **www.canadianspeakers.org** , to learn more about our organization, what's happening in your local chapter or what's new in the speaking industry. Whether you are a fellow speaker, a journalist, an organization in need of expert resources, a meeting planner searching for a presenter, or a bureau scouting for skilled speakers, we welcome you to our community.

Linda Tarrant, CSP, HoF
2003 CAPS National President

Foreword

Where was this book twenty years ago? If you are an established speaker or an aspiring speaker you must read this book.

Where else can you get detailed information on how to excel as a trainer or a keynoter with Cheryl Cran, CSP Candidate, or learn how to leverage the Internet to increase profit in your speaking practice with Dr. Feel Good? So many great tips on how to succeed in the speaking business have been jam-packed into this book that you might want to take it slowly. But take it!

The pros from the Vancouver chapter of CAPS are among the best in the world, including Linda Edgecombe, Margaret Hope, Geoffrey Lane, Sherrin Western, Elaine Allison, David Granirer, Carla Rieger, Abegael Fisher-Lang, Lorne Kelton and Lynn Robinson.

Regardless of where you are at in this wonderful business of speaking this book will leverage your success immensely.

Every speaker starts out with a dream—a dream about making a difference in the world. That dream begins to become a reality as each speaker's passion turns into a business. The transition from passion to business can be difficult and this book will help to ease the pain.

This book will remind long-time speakers where we need to re-focus our energy, and we may learn a thing or two that we may either have forgotten or just didn't know.

Get all of your friends, family and colleagues to buy this book. It will inspire and motivate all speakers to go out there and do more good in the world.

Peter Legge, LLD, CPAE, HoF, CSP

Getting Started

by Elaine Allison

You may be an accomplished speaker looking for further insight in certain areas. You may just be starting in the business or have made some strides into the area of speaking, facilitating or training. No matter what stage you are at, the following will give you a brief outline of what you need to get started. In this chapter you will review many aspects of setting up your business in one of the most exciting careers I've encountered.

I have broken the chapter into three areas that any businessperson must focus on to ensure success. Not paying attention to one of these can result in fatal flaws in a business venture. These three areas are marketing, operations and finance.

Speakers come into the profession in many ways. Some have been training, facilitating or consulting in the corporate world. Some are celebrities, authors or experts in their fields. However, if you have made the decision, I would advise you to join the Canadian Association of Professional Speakers (CAPS), the National Speakers Association (NSA) or the International Federation of Professional Speakers (IFPS) if you have not already done so. In these organizations you will find people who share a common goal, and a way to remove the isolation often felt by many speakers, trainers and facilitators. You will learn many aspects of building your business in the industry. Competitors may appear, but I guarantee you will meet far more friends who support your goals, pick you up when your last engagement flopped and offer you answers to your most difficult challenges. You don't have to do this alone.

Marketing and Your Business Model

The first item you must establish as you start or build your business is to define who and what your business is about. You must have a plan. Determine the answers to these seven questions. Grab a piece of paper and start writing. Blanks or places where you are not sure of the answers are indications that additional research is required.

- What is your area of expertise?
- Who will you speak to?
- How large is your target market? How often do they meet? How often will they require your services?
- Where will you find information to help you market to them?
- Why will they want this information?

- How will it help them?

- What products will you offer that will supplement your speaking business? (e.g. books, tapes, CDs, videos)

- How are you different from or better than three direct competitors?

You can start finding out the answers to these questions by asking friends, family or those who have seen you speak. Find out what you are good at. Make a list of everything you've accomplished in your life, including your education and experience. (Make sure you include life experiences also.) You will need this list when you are ready to develop marketing materials like a one-pager, bio and introductions. These are discussed in following chapters.

The next step is to visit speakers' bureau web sites and the NSA (**www.nsaspeaker.org**) and CAPS (**www.canadianspeakers.org**) web sites. All have speaker listings by topic, area of expertise and geographic location. From there you can usually find links to other pertinent web sites. Some of the bureau sites include fee ranges. When you visit, find your competitors and note everything you can about them. What is the quality of their videos, web sites, biographies and other marketing pieces? How do you compare? How will you differentiate yourself? Do not get discouraged. It takes time and effort to build your business and the items you will need to support it. The more you learn about the marketplace and your competitors the better prepared you will be. Once you have decided on your target market, see our chapters on branding and marketing.

Operations: Setting Up Your Business

Most professional speakers, trainers and facilitators are self-employed. You will need to determine if you will operate as a sole proprietor, or incorporate. It is a good idea to get a free half-hour consultation with a lawyer and an accountant to determine your best option.

Self-employment also means you often start your speaking business without staff. You will require a room, usually in your home. If you are lucky enough to have office space it is best to balance the cost versus the convenience. I personally work from my home and find that most of my work is conducted at a client site, hotel meeting room or even at coffee shops. Having a home office allows me to balance both my career and home life. The relationships I have built at CAPS have assisted me in combating the challenge of isolation often found by self-employed or home office entrepreneurs.

When you set up your office you should ensure you put good systems and equipment in place. Here are a few things you will need to do if you are just starting out. Do a cost analysis on each of these items (including the marketing items mentioned in a following chapter). You will need this information when we get to finance and setting fees.

Equipment

- Computer, possibly a laptop and projection unit
- Software, including presentation and database management software

- Colour printer, scanner, photocopier, fax machine
- High speed Internet access, domain name and e-mail address with domain name extension
- Separate telephone line, fax line, and in most cases a cellular phone

Critical Documents You Need to Design

- Fax cover page
- Sample contract templates
- Letterhead (I design my own in Microsoft Word™)
- Professionally designed business card
- Invoice template
- Client and potential client database (see chapter on using the Internet)
- Bio, introductions and one-pagers (see other chapters)
- Pre-program questionnaire
- Checklists for working with meeting planners (you will develop your own system for this, but typically it will cover things such as room set-up, handouts, AV requirements, travel schedule, location and times, confirmations, etc.)
- Visas for international work

Note: If you plan on selling products you will have several more documents and systems to set up, such as an order entry process.

Other Operational Systems

- Time management, scheduling and tracking system, especially if you are going for a CSP designation (visit the CAPS web site for more information)

- Travel and scheduling system (for instance, a good way to get maps to find speaking locations is to try **mapquest.com** and click on "Get Driving Directions". Type in starting and destination addresses.)

- Accounting system (see finance section)

Finance

Setting Up Your Accounting System

One of the most critical items to set up is a solid accounting system. Do it right from the beginning. There is nothing worse than handing your accountant a shoebox at year-end. You may decide to set up your own accounting system or contract someone to do your posting and year-end accounting. Taxes must be paid on a regular basis and it is imperative to have good counsel to ensure you obtain the best tax advantages from the start. Bookkeeping and accounting were areas where I decided I needed the most help. From the beginning I found someone to set up and post my receipts, invoices and payments on a regular basis. Now that a solid system has been set up I could do the work myself, but I feel it is well worth it to get someone else to do a task I find tedious. Each year I review my business and accounting practices with my accountant, who directs me into the most profitable areas of my practice. This extra set of eyes helps me find hidden opportunities and can point out costly errors. I feel it is one reason I am still in business today.

Setting Fees

I have always been a huge champion of budgeting and forecasting. I needed to see how much everything was going to cost me and compare it to how much business I would have to bring in. Budgeting and forecasting also help you set fees that cover your costs and allow you to put some money aside to build your business and develop as a speaker year after year. Work out your costs and determine your fee range, and revenues if you have product, then determine how many speaking engagements (and products) you need to sell to cover those costs, pay yourself a salary and have money left over to purchase items to continue to grow your business. The first few years are the hardest.

Each year I compare my actual costs and revenues against the previous year and build new forecasts for the upcoming year. Each year I get better at controlling my expenditures and therefore enhancing the profit needed to continue in business. I always leave money for professional development like attending NSA and CAPS conferences, where you learn from other professionals.

Lines of Credit

One of the most critical elements a small businessperson often omits is obtaining a line of credit to assist with cash flow. A line of credit attached to your business account can be your lifeline as you wait for cheques to come in or to cover slower months. Too many businesses fail to judge the amount they really need to carry themselves. One warning in this area: ensure you follow your budget or forecast. The money in a line of credit is not there to spend just because it is available to you. This is not your money. It is actually the financial institution's, and they want it back. Use it wisely to cover your costs while you are getting started, waiting for known receivables or to develop your business. Just ensure you have a plan in place for where and how the business (also known as revenue) will come. Many a well-intended entrepreneur has underestimated this requirement.

Putting It Together

The next page shows the simplest formula I can think of for those of you who have had no accounting experience. When you sit down to determine your fees, and the number of engagements you will need to survive, you will soon see why I have broken the process of running a business down into three integrated components.

In other words, if you don't market or put money into marketing, you won't get engagements. If you don't have solid operational systems in place that save you precious time, you will run out of time to conduct business. Lastly, if you don't watch your money, or finances, you will run out of it as you build your business. It is a delicate balance.

Run Your Numbers

Money In (annual)

Annual revenue from products $ _____

Speaking fee per engagement $ _____

  x engagements/year   = $ _____

                                     = $ _____

Total Revenue

Subtract

Money Out (annual)

Equipment $ _____

Personal development $ _____

Marketing $ _____

Accounting/Legal $ _____

Supplies $ _____

Salary $ _____

                                   =

Total Costs

Total Costs $ _____ — **Total Revenue** $ _____ = $ _____

Profit or Loss

I wish you the best in your business venture. I hope you find it one of the most exhilarating experiences of your life. Hang on for the ride and I hope you enjoy the many tips, ideas and thoughts shared in this book. I only wish I had found the wisdom provided in this book sooner. I know it will save you time, money and heartache as you move forward with your own speaking practice.

Elaine Allison
Positive Presentations Plus Inc.
2241 Stafford Ave.
Port Coquitlam, BC V3C 4X5
P: 604-723-7774
F: 604-944-7186
eallison@presentationsplusinc.com
www.presentationsplusinc.com

About Elaine Allison

Elaine Allison, better known as **The Business Attendant**, is an international speaker and successful business development consultant. Her entrepreneurial flair was recognized when she received the Visions of Excellence Entrepreneur of the Year Award in the consulting category in 2002.

Elaine obtained her education in correctional services and became one of Canada's first female prison officers in an all-male maximum security prison at the age of nineteen. She moved on to the turbulent airline industry and the aggressive financial and insurance services business, and endured the spiraling technology sector prior to building her own speaking and consulting practice, **Positive Presentations Plus Inc.**, in 1999.

Bored with wearing the corporate uniform while speaking, Elaine began to create themes for her events and turned to costumes and characterizations to make her point. You can visit her web site for more information, at **www.presentationsplusinc.com** .

Elaine holds a CAPS Professional designation and is working towards her CSP. She will be the president of the BC chapter in 2004.

Elaine is the proud daughter of a mother who has lived with diabetes since 1939. A percentage of Elaine's speaking engagement fees is donated to the Juvenile Diabetes Research Foundation.

Sales and Marketing: Leaving No Stone Unturned

by Lorne Kelton

Your sales and marketing strategies must be based upon, and work in harmony with, your goals as a professional speaker. Until you know where you are versus where you want to be, there is no point in spending time, money, and energy pursuing an undefined strategy.

Assuming that you have defined your core offerings, have branded your identity accordingly and have identified your target market(s), it is now time to present yourself—the package—to that market. As an independent information practitioner, you have limited time, resources, and expertise to effectively tackle the plethora of opportunities that exist. Five strategies, however, that must be considered include the following.

A Professionally Designed Web Site

An Internet web presence that aligns with, and adheres to, your core values, products, and services is indispensable. The site must be clear, comprehensive, and incorporate intuitive navigation. Your web site should be the focal point around which your other efforts revolve. Why? Because, given the ubiquity of the World Wide Web, it is one of the strongest and most cost-effective marketing tools ever created. It allows around-the-clock access, in real time, to information about your products and services as a speaker or trainer. Your web site, when effectively designed and hosted, serves as a mouthpiece representing you in your absence. Your web site can also serve as a revenue generator to supplement your speaking and/or training revenues.

Be mindful that most clients and audience members have come to expect a web presence to go along with the "live show". Without that presence you may lose a key opportunity to remain accessible to your paying customers beyond the speaking engagement.

Well-Researched, Well-Written Materials

Along with your speaking credentials, you need to develop and hone your writing skills. There is an increasing expectation in the marketplace that professional speakers not only write, but write well. Well-researched and well-written materials are vital. You can no longer rely on your platform mechanics and personal style to get by. Unfortunately, the sheer volume of trite and vapid material spewed forth by unprepared speakers is atrocious.

Since content is king, you need to have well-thought out and well-researched written materials to enhance and support your speaking initiatives. It's also good for business since your written materials can serve as fodder for your newsletters, e-zines, or a potential book. If you want exposure for your written articles or columns beyond your web site and speaking venues, consider looking at **WritersMarket.com**, which has a searchable database of more than 4,000 publishers and literary agents to whom you can submit your work.

Public Seminars and Freebies: Highly Effective Loss Leaders

Another marketing consideration should be public seminars and complimentary speaking engagements. Though these strategies may not make money up front, they often lead to booked engagements at a later date. The trick with public seminars and other "freebies" is to ensure that you have targeted an audience that has the potential to provide a return on your investment. This return may include letters of reference, testimonials, networking opportunities, and the chance to return to that same group on a paid basis in the future. Word of mouth spreads very quickly and it only takes one key decisionmaker in your audience to get your speaking ball rolling. Being highly selective about the groups you choose will improve the odds of success in harnessing this valuable tool to build your business.

Product Development

You want your audience to take a piece of you away with them at the end of the keynote or seminar. To do this you will need one or more of the following: audio tapes, videotapes, CDs, subscriptions, e-zines, and books. These all take on lives of their own and perpetuate your marketing strategies. They also require a lot of time and preparation and should never be an afterthought.

Look to your local CAPS or NSA chapter for professionals who have expertise in the kind of product development that you require. You will save time, money, and heartache by investing up front in these critical residual revenue generators rather than producing them ad hoc. Once developed, they should be proactively promoted on your web site as an extension of yourself and your business.

Media Attention

Media spots can create priceless "buzz" to raise awareness, perpetuate your brand, and enhance credibility. This may mean articles in local or national newspapers and magazines. It may mean being a guest on a radio or television show. The harder you work at getting yourself "out there" the luckier you will be in securing media opportunities.

Your sales and marketing success will be a direct result of the focus you bring to bear on your speaking business. This means defining your professional goals and designing a roadmap to get there in a defined period of time. The suggestions proposed here are designed to assist you in reaching those goals expeditiously.

Lorne Kelton
ThinkShift Technologies Inc.
9133 Evancio Cres.
Richmond, BC V7E 5J2
P: 604-277-9911
F: 604-304-0141
lorne@thinkshift.com
www.thinkshift.com

About Lorne Kelton

For over twenty years, Lorne Kelton, founder of **ThinkShift Technologies Inc.**, has helped corporations and small businesses implement innovative learning strategies for performance breakthroughs. Lorne's eclectic professional experience is manifested in his signature speaking themes, which include "Unlocking the Power of Passion", "Emotivity at Work", and "Intensive Care for Small Business". Lorne brings a powerful combination of street smarts and contrary thinking to all of his presentations, leaving his audiences stirred and looking at their personal and professional lives in a whole new light. Lorne is a Professional member of the Canadian Association of Professional Speakers.

Create and Market Your Authentic Brand!

by Sherrin Western

Is your presentation as a speaker congruent with the presentation of your printed and online marketing materials? Whether you have books, tapes, videos, compact discs, business cards, one-sheets, multimedia presentations or a web site, these marketing tools leave an impression about you and your business with your audiences and clients. Is it an accurate impression? Is the impression you leave a true reflection of you? Audiences and clients deserve to know that your package is in sync with who you are and what you deliver.

Without honest evaluation of who you are and what you deliver, you risk confusing your prospective customers with contradictory image-messages, which ultimately means less business. I call such contradictions "disconnected image".

When I attended my first Canadian Association of Professional Speakers (CAPS) convention, I saw this confusion with image demonstrated repeatedly. I picked up a brochure for a speaker I had not heard of from the product and marketing table. It practically jumped into my hands because it was of such poor quality. You know the kind—bad photocopying, way too much small type, poorly folded on plain, really flimsy paper. It was easy to discount this speaker as unprofessional based on the impression her brochure left, so you can imagine my surprise and curiosity when I found that she was to be a concurrent session speaker the next day. Of course, I made sure I attended her session, and couldn't have been more delighted by what a great presenter she was. Her brochure was doing her a great disservice! How many potential clients saw her brochure before they saw her speak, and immediately discounted her skills as a speaker because of the impression the brochure left? The sad part is that we will never know the answer to this question.

Could this be happening to you? Unfortunately for some speakers, the answer is yes.

Have you ever heard the statement, "you ARE your business"? This statement implies that you must be your best—always—because you are representing your business every minute of every day! This couldn't be more true for self-employed speakers. How you manage your behaviour on and off the platform is not only what people notice, it is what they will remember.

When a group of my speaking colleagues and I returned from a conference, we got another amazing example of a fellow speaker's disconnected image. We attended a concurrent session where the speaker opened with an entertaining story about losing her luggage on the trip to the conference. The session she delivered was jam-packed with quality information and tips—everyone left her session feeling they got value.

Now, fast forward to our cab ride to the airport at the conclusion of the conference. The cab driver struck up conversation with us and when he found out we were at the speakers' conference, he told a very interesting story about the presenter who had lost her luggage. He had been her cab driver and described her as aggressive, unkind, demanding and certainly ungrateful for any assistance he tried to give her in her time of frustration. The picture he painted for us was completely contrary to what we had seen the previous day.

Our greatest lesson from the conference happened right there in the taxi. You must be authentic on and off the platform. As we learned from the cab driver, it all counts! Your ability on the platform, your marketing and your demeanour off the platform all form your reputation in this business, or in any business for that matter.

Make sure your style as a speaker is represented in your marketing materials. If, for example, you speak to the corporate market and your style is conservative and formal, your marketing materials should reflect this. A fun, lighthearted, and colourful marketing package would misrepresent you to your prospective clients. You are unique and your style of presenting is unique; therefore your marketing materials should also be unique and reflective of you.

Understand Your Current Reality; Create Your Future Vision

So how do you articulate your uniqueness? By using a process that gets you to really analyze yourself and your speaking business: where you are now to where you want to be in the future.

This needs to be undertaken with as many facts and as much data as you can compile. It is impossible to understand and confidently convey your uniqueness if you don't know what else is going on in the marketplace around you. Although the questions might seem daunting at first, it is important to answer them as honestly as you can. Here are the questions we use with our clients that help to get to the root of what their business is all about.

Brand Exploration Questions

- Exactly what kind of work do you do?
- What kind of product/service do you provide?
- What kind of problems do you solve for your clients?
- Who are your current clients?
- Who is your ideal client/industry?
- What kind of work do you want to be doing in the future?
- What do you stand for? What do you value?
- Describe your personality and the "personality" of your company

- What are your personal strengths and weaknesses? What opportunities exist for you personally? What threatens your success?

- What strengths and weaknesses does your business have? What opportunities are there for your business? What threatens your business success?

- Who are your direct competitors? What makes you different from them?

- What do your customers remember about you?

- What keeps your customers coming back?

- What makes you credible in your business?

- What will your life look like in five years? Ten years?

- What will you be best known or remembered for in five years? Ten years?

- What does your business look like in five years? Ten years?

- What does your exit strategy look like for the business?

Once you have answered these questions, you begin to get a picture of your current reality and what you want your future to look like. Armed with this information, you can begin to create your authentic brand.

Create Your Ideal Target Market

A critical requirement for any business to market its product or service effectively is to know as much as possible about its target market (ideal client) as possible. Take some time to get clarity on the attributes of your target market before you begin seeking them out and marketing to them.

I liken this to looking for a needle in a haystack. If asked to find the needle, many people would begin looking, grumbling all the while about how hard it was to find such a small item in such a large haystack. In contrast, a wise person might ask a few questions to maximize his or her efforts before beginning the search, such as, "What colour is the needle? How long is it? What material is it made of?" Confirming facts instead of running off armed only with assumptions about what the needle looks like makes it much easier to find the needle. What if you found out that the needle was purple, twelve inches long and made of melamine?

The same is true of finding customers. If you know what types of customers you are looking for, it will be much easier to find them. What industry are they in? How many employees do they have? How long have they been in business? What is their reputation? What is their annual revenue? Who is the decisionmaker for your type of product or service? The more you know about your target market, the easier it will be to market to them.

The Power of Target Market Focus

Speakers who clearly understand the target market they are focusing on have a huge advantage when it comes to marketing. They know what their target market reads, the types of associations they belong to, what their industry challenges are, what is common among the companies in their target market, and much more. Knowing this kind of information helps you decide how to market your products or services effectively. It allows you to "speak the language" in all of your marketing. From your brochures to your web site, your language can be specific to the commonalities of your target market. Obviously, this ultimately means financial savings. Because you have focused your efforts, you don't have to have different sets of materials.

Marketing Materials and Your Business Image

Every speech you give, every letter you write, every e-mail you answer and every telephone call you make is either building your business image or damaging it. Which is it in your case? Here are some simple guidelines you can follow to ensure you are proactively building your image.

Be consistent! It sets you apart. A very easy way to separate you and your business from others in the marketplace is to be consistent. Consistency with your brand across all media is a big step and demonstrates stability to prospective and current clients. When they recognize something as yours, you are brand-building through consistency.

Think of the big brands you see every day. How did they get to be so recognizable? By being absolutely committed to representing their brand consistently. You can do that too. Use the same colours and typeface for both your print materials and web site. Have a unique logo created for your business and put it on everything you create and give out. Ensure that your e-mail address is consistent with your web site address. What does it say about you or your company when your e-mail address is from one of the big providers that issues free e-mail addresses? Your e-mail address format should be similar to the following: **yourname@yourcompany.xxx** (a plethora of extensions are possible—.com, .ca, .net, .org, .biz, just to name a few). And your web site address should be **www.yourcompany.xxx** .

From how you answer the phone, send e-mail and return calls to how and when you invoice, everything is part of the consistency customers look for from their service providers. When they get consistency, they feel that the company is reliable. Reliability drives strong relationships that eventually grow into loyalty because the company can be counted on consistently.

Keep information current. Have you ever received a business card from someone that has one or more items scratched out? Have you put a new address label on your brochure because you have moved since you printed it? Both of these actions are saying something about the business, and it is not usually positive. Demonstrate your commitment to your professional image by ensuring that whatever you give out is current. It shows people that you pay attention to detail, and that is a great quality for any business to have.

It is critical that all contact information (mailing address, phone numbers, e-mail addresses, etc.) be accurate 100 percent of the time. If people have difficulty tracking you down because they have old information, they will most likely give up and search for someone else before they find you.

The minute that any information is out of date on printed materials, it is time to throw those materials into the recycling bin and get new ones printed. If you have a large quantity of material that is now out of date that you can't bear to throw away, speak to your graphic designer. There may be an innovative way to update the information and keep the integrity of the printed material intact. You can also check with your designer or printer for advice on smaller print runs if you know your information may change. These are some of the options that you will want to understand prior to making your print decisions.

Review your topics, testimonials and client list regularly. Ensure you keep your client list current by adding new clients as you work with them. I also recommend updating the testimonials you request and receive so the ones you use are as current as possible. If all your testimonials are five years old, what does that say about your company?

The same goes for your topics. It is critical that only the topics you want to present are included in your package. There is nothing worse than having a client ask for a topic in your package, only to be told that you no longer do that presentation! Keep your information current.

In the speaking industry, your photo will always be part of your marketing. Be sure that your photo is flattering and current. If your photo is more than two years old, you may be misrepresenting yourself. You never want to be in a position where the client or meeting planner is expecting someone much younger. Do you ever feel like everyone else looks older, but you have stayed the same? I am sure we all have felt that way at some point, but it is likely not the truth. Keep updating your photo to ensure you are promoting the current "you". It is an important part of keeping your brand authentic.

Good design and printing don't need to break the bank. You have many opportunities to maximize your financial investment when creating your identity and marketing package. By using colour, paper stocks and print quantities creatively, and keeping open dialogues with your designer and printer, you can get more than you might at first think possible. A common item that many speakers develop for their presentation packages is letterhead that can double as a shell for your topic sheets, bio and client list as well. You merely overprint your information on the pre-printed letterhead, making it easy to update the information regularly.

Whenever possible, find out from your target market and clients what form of communication they prefer. If you know they primarily rely on electronic communication, you might produce very little print material and focus on electronic versions of your package. If you are working with speakers' bureaus, be sure you have materials produced that are bureau-friendly, which means your contact information is not included.

Some other tips to remember when creating your materials:

- White space is king—less copy has more impact on the reader.

- Write from a benefit-and-outcome point of view. What does the customer really want to know?

- Accuracy—more than one set of eyes is invaluable when proofing.

Craft your image on the web. Before you race to have a web site developed for your business, it is imperative to understand how a web site fits into your overall marketing plan. Without knowing this, you can make some poor decisions about your online presence.

You must make it easy for customers to visit your site and get what they want. Poorly organized and cluttered sites can scare visitors away. Having the site designed and programmed effectively is the first step, but your real work begins once the site is live. Visitors expect information on web sites to be updated regularly and return more often if it is.

The importance of bringing customers back cannot be overstated. Successful web sites create reasons for people to return to the site. All printed materials and articles must have your web site address included to ensure you are taking every opportunity to send people to your site. But you must ask yourself what they will get once they go there. Are you providing value on your site? Are you updating your information regularly? It damages your image to have great information such as your speaking calendar on the site if it has obviously not been updated for a period of time: for example, if the last entry in your speaking calendar was for the summer of 2002! People will either conclude that you don't speak very often, or that you don't take the time to update your site.

In Summary

Creating and marketing your authentic brand takes focus, but it is well worth the effort. Ask yourself with regard to all your marketing initiatives, "Will what I am about to do help or hinder my image?" You can then adjust your action so that the answer to the question is always "help".

Sherrin Western
SHERVIN communications Inc.
Ste. 101, 8557 Government Rd.
Burnaby, BC V3N 4S9
P: 604-422-0174
F: 604-422-0175
sherrin@goshervin.com
www.goshervin.com

About Sherrin Western

Sherrin is an expert in brand image, marketing and customer relationships and brings her knowledge to many organizations with keynote addresses and workshops nationally.

Sherrin owns a graphic design and marketing studio, **SHERVIN communications**, with her husband Kevin. They work with clients to help articulate and honour clients' unique "brand" image, which includes marketing consulting and visual representation of corporate identity to all supporting promotional literature.

Her passionate and honest style is refreshing and leaves people with a real and practical understanding of the content she presents. Sherrin knows that for the message to be believable the person delivering it must also be. She has an inquisitive yet friendly manner and seeks to approach issues from the customer point of view—always!

As a volunteer, Sherrin has been involved with victim assistance, community policing, the 1991 and 1997 BC Summer Games, and the youth mentorship program. She is currently National Chapter Liaison for Canadian Women in Communications and Immediate Past President of the Canadian Association of Professional Speakers in BC. Sherrin is also a member of the Vancouver and Burnaby Boards of Trade.

Sherrin has appeared on television and has been interviewed by the *Globe and Mail*, *BC Business*, *Business in Vancouver* and other BC publications regarding running and marketing a small business. Her focus in life is to enjoy the great people in her life, commit to lifelong learning, serve her community and help people be their unique and authentic selves.

For her dedication and effort, she has been included in the *Who's Who of Canadian Women* and *Who's Who in Canadian Business* publications. Sherrin was also awarded Woman of Distinction honours in Burnaby in 1997. And she was one of twenty finalists for the Influential Woman in Business award for 2000 in Vancouver.

Create a Demo Video That Works

by Sherrin Western

If you have ever spoken with a bureau representative, meeting planner or client who regularly books speakers, you know that they will almost always request a copy of your promo or demo video. Previewing speakers' videos is a regular part of their decisionmaking process, and without one you will be at a great disadvantage. The decisionmakers want to know that you are a good speaker, that audiences enjoy your presentations, and that you are an expert on your topic. All of these points must be visible in your demo video.

So how can you produce a demo video that will help you market yourself effectively? First, hire a videographer who wants to really understand your style as a speaker before he or she shows up to videotape your sessions. Videographers should understand as much as possible about how you deliver your presentations—it makes them more aware of what to look for while taping. You should be very clear about what you want to have taped during your session. It is not just a case of "point and shoot".

Critical Elements to Capture

When you go to the effort and expense to have someone tape your sessions, it is imperative that you capture a few key elements.

The audience. It is always a plus for viewers to see people in the audience laughing and enjoying themselves. If you can get two video cameras with two microphones to record your session (or you have a great videographer who can move around the room effectively), it will help to capture the true atmosphere of the event by ensuring that you and your audience are heard and taped.

Some close-ups of you during your performance so the viewer can see your facial expressions and hand gestures. A video doesn't present you as well if the camera is in the back of a large room and you just look like some tiny figure up front.

A good-looking room. If you are presenting in a tiny rundown classroom, chances are that the video will not be as positive as it can be. Although good videographers can do amazing things, it can be tough to hide a poor room. Choose the sessions you want to have taped carefully.

As many different speeches as possible. If you can schedule the videographer to tape "ideal" sections, or all, of three or four different presentations you give, you are not only sure to get some good segments for your video, but it also shows the viewer that you have done more than one presentation.

You, telling your unique stories! If you want viewers to hire you, they have to know that your stories are yours. They don't want to hire a speaker who tells the same stories as other speakers. Seeing you present unique material from your life experience and perspective is very compelling for viewers.

Your personality and style. Clients are looking for you to be your best you. Let it show through!

As little date-specific information as possible. If you include a clip making some reference to the year (for example, "in 2003 we have seen a change in that belief") the presentation appears dated. A viewer watching that clip in 2006 might be distracted from your delivery by thinking about the age of the video, even though it may still be relevant and useable in 2006. If there are no references to the date, no one will even question it.

Video Duration

Although there are demo videos of all lengths out there, I have been told by people in the broadcast industry as well as in the bureau world that ten to fifteen minutes is preferred. The people who hire speakers are busy, so we need to give them everything they are looking for in a maximum of fifteen minutes. If you want the viewer to see a complete speech, add it at the conclusion of the demo video with some kind of audio or graphic introduction.

Video, CD, Web or Audio?

In the past all demos were VHS videotapes or audio cassettes, but that is changing. We notice in the multimedia work we do that more and more people in many industries other than speaking are moving to CD and web-based video. So when you get a video produced, ensure that you get the video captured as a computer video file as well. This enables you to put some of your video on your web site as short clips so that visitors to your site can see examples of you speaking. Since the popularity of the multimedia CD format continues to grow, you can also produce your demo on CD. You may want to create some variety on your demo by using audio clips as voice-overs with some still photos of yourself.

At the Production Stage

When your demo is being edited and produced you may want to add some or all of the following.

Adding graphic elements helps connect the video clips that you will be using. Just be sure that your demo doesn't become overloaded with graphics so that the focus moves away from your speaking.

Testimonials from satisfied clients can be included as audio clips or added as written quotes on-screen. Endorsements must be real and compelling! Ensure you get your clients' approval before you use their testimonials.

The look and feel of your marketing materials should extend to your video. It should be easy to recognize that this tape is yours—by both the tape and by the sleeve or packaging that it comes in. Make sure you label both. Remember, the viewers of these videos may have many to look at. How easy is it for them to identify yours? Because the demo will often be sent out with your package, you will maximize your professional brand image if everything looks like it belongs together.

A list of "other topics presented" is useful. This can help viewers see that you cover a variety of topics. If they like your style, they may be interested in knowing this type of information.

Include a detailed version of your biography. This bio should be more detailed than the one in the demo. It can be included at the end as a source of supplemental information.

If you are having a video produced, ensure you keep it bureau-friendly. This means no contact information. You may have a line in the video that says something like, "Call the number on the video label for booking information". That way you have a choice about whose number will be put on the label, yours or the bureau's, depending on the situation.

An Extension of
Your Marketing Efforts

Your demo video is a very important part of your marketing effort. Therefore you will want to give thought to how it can work best for you. How you distribute it is as important as how you get it produced. A great video poorly distributed is not going to help grow your business. And a poor video with good distribution will not grow your business either. The key factor to maximizing the value from producing a video is to make it as easy as possible for people to see clips of you speaking, in whatever medium they find most comfortable.

The video you have produced doesn't need to be loaded with bells and whistles to be effective. It needs to have great clips of you, put together elegantly and distributed to the right people, so that your demo video is as professional as you are!

Sherrin Western
SHERVIN Communications Inc.
Ste. 101, 8557 Government Rd.
Burnaby, BC V3N 4S9
P: 604-422-0174
F: 604-422-0175
sherrin@goshervin.com
www.goshervin.com

About Sherrin Western

Sherrin is an expert in brand image, marketing and customer relationships and brings her knowledge to many organizations with keynote addresses and workshops nationally.

Sherrin owns a graphic design and marketing studio, **SHERVIN communications**, with her husband Kevin. They work with clients to help articulate and honour clients' unique "brand" image, which includes marketing consulting and visual representation of corporate identity to all supporting promotional literature.

Please see page 31 for a complete biography.

How the Internet Saves Speakers Time and Money

by Natalie Forstbauer

My expertise in the Internet and technology came out of a deep curiosity and yearning to understand how I could leverage my time, business and speaking career with technology and the Internet. I literally devoted two years to studying and applying various forms of Internet marketing, and testing the many software products available.

It all began when I discovered how easy it was to send an e-mail. Prior to sending my first e-mail I was terrified of computers. Now I am a bit of a techie. In my spare time I play with technology, programming languages and the newest Internet marketing strategies.

A big challenge in writing this chapter is that much of the information I am about to give you changes as fast as people change their socks. What I say about the subject today could be irrelevant tomorrow. To combat part of this I am going to give you a link to my web site that will connect you to web sites and experts that keep up on technology and the Internet.

I source experts and mentors to keep me up to speed with the Internet and technology. One chapter is far too little space for me to do justice to the amount of information I want to share with you. To keep things simple, I have created a special resource page on my web site with the hottest links and resources in Internet marketing and technology. Some of these links lead to products and e-books you can purchase, but many of the links have freebies, too—free e-zines and reports with loads of value. The resource page is **www.dare2feel.com/speakers.html** .

Look Professional on the Internet

Get a Domain Name That Rocks

A domain name is what people use to locate you on the Internet. For example, my main domain names are **natalieforstbauer.com** or **dare2feel.com**. The entire "www.yourname.com" address is called an URL.

As a speaker the best domain name is your name. If you have a trademark name you can use that too. In the speaking industry, it is said that using your own name is the best choice. Personally, I have registered many domain names. It helps people find me.

If you register another domain name you can have it point to your main web site. This is called "forwarding" a domain name. I forward many of my domains to my main web site. For example, my main web site is **www.dare2feel.com**.

Currently **www.natalieforstbauer.com** and **www.myzenergy.com** are forwarded to my main site. Whether people are looking for Natalie J. Forstbauer the speaker or Zenergy, my online health portal, they can always find me at **www.dare2feel.com**.

It is possible to have many URLs pointed to one web site. Forwarding is particularly great for speakers who want to have only one web site, but who want to own URLs incorporating both their company name and personal name. Look for domain forwarding when you purchase your domain. Sometimes it is free.

When you have a domain name, put it on everything: your business cards, flyers, bookmarks, books, and at the end of articles you write. Tell everyone about it.

Domain Name Registration

Today it costs pennies to register a domain name. All you have to do is go to a web site that registers domain names and follow the instructions to register your domain. If the name you have chosen is taken, the web site will often give you a list of alternative names that are close to yours. I have listed some great domain registration companies on my resource page. One of my favourite places at the moment is **www.godaddy.com** . For just $8.95 US you can have the domain name of your choice, if it is available.

Hosting Your Domain

It is important to host your domain with a service provider that has 99.9 percent "up time".

That means your web site will never or rarely be "down", or unavailable. Hosting companies charge anywhere from $5 a month to hundreds of dollars a month. A good way to find a host is to ask around, or research web host ratings on the Internet. I find it best to work with a host company that is local. It supports local business and if anything happens you can more easily track them down. Questions to ask are:

- What is your up time?
- Do you have multiple or redundant backbones?
- What is your maximum and average connection speed?
- How many e-mail accounts are included and how do I set up my e-mail accounts?
- How many megabytes of storage are included? (Get 50 MB or more.)
- Are auto-responders included? (You want these.)
- What type of support do you provide? (Personal service is important.)

E-mail Etiquette

Have you ever been added to someone's newsletter or e-zine without your permission? I have, and it is annoying. It is unprofessional, invasive and an intrusion on privacy. Only add people to your database with their permission.

Return e-mails within twenty-four hours. People are used to slow return e-mails. It impresses them when you get back to them quickly.

Always begin your e-mails with a greeting, or the person's name. The only time I break this rule is when I am working on a project with someone I know very well and we are almost having a conversation.

Your E-mail Signature

Include a signature (called a sig) at the end of your e-mails. Typically an e-mail signature will include:

Name
Title
Company name
Slogan
Telephone number
Web site URL
Professional achievements

It is best to keep your e-mail signature to a maximum of seven lines. It is okay if your signature is longer, but make it interesting. Most people will read your signature at least once. That is the goal. As a rule, always include a link to your web site in your signature.

My e-mail signature reads:

Natalie J Forstbauer
aka "Dr. Feel Good"
Author, Speaker, Consultant
Tel. 1.604.737.3632 (in Vancouver BC)
Toll Free. 1.877.559.3273
http://www.dare2feel.com

You are invited to sign up for Natalie's Free E-Zine on Health-E Tips and Workplace Wellness. Go To: http://www.dare2feel.com

Wrap Your Text

Have you ever received an e-mail that looks like this?

"Hello Tammy, it was great to see you yesterday, I am happy to hear
you are doing what you love to do. The course you are taking is
awesome. Best of luck to you!"

The e-mail looks the way it does because the sender's e-mail "client" program (Outlook, Netscape, Eudora or whatever the sender uses to write and send e-mail) is set to wrap the lines in a message at a predetermined number of characters, but yours wraps at a higher number or not at all. One character equals one space.

Typically sixty characters is the lowest a person will set an e-mail client to wrap. Make a point of wrapping your text at sixty characters in the Settings dialogue box on your e-mail client. If you do not know how to do this, check in the Help menu or add a hard return by pressing Enter after every sixty characters or fewer. I always set my e-mail client program to fifty-nine characters for outgoing messages to be on the safe side. When I send out e-mail, recipients will never get a broken e-mail like the example above unless their e-mail clients are set to fewer than fifty-nine characters, which is highly unlikely.

Web Site Design

Keep It Simple

Did you know that web sites with complex graphics, Java or Flash programming and other high tech bells and whistles will often rank lower on search engines than a web site with the exact same content created in plain HTML? It's true.

Why? Search engines like to keep things simple. "Spiders" or "bots" (search programs) are launched by search engines to look for pages to rank. They will skip over web sites that are too complex and go straight to more simple HTML pages, thus ranking the simple pages higher. The end result is that simple web pages are often ranked higher than flashy web sites.

When I consult with speakers who want to build a web site I encourage them to keep it simple. Yes, bells and whistles are nice to look at, but they do nothing for your ranking on search engines. The web sites at the top of search engines are the ones that get visited. If a web site is lower than the top ten in search engine listings it is often overlooked. See the "Getting Found" section to learn how to be at the top.

If it is not important to you to be at the top of search engines and having a flashy cool web site is more important, then by all means go for it! Just remember to drive traffic to your web site with alternative marketing techniques.

Of course, you don't have to rely on search engine submission to get your web site to rank high. You can also pay to be ranked at the top of a search engine. People can opt to accept "pay-per-click", sponsor links, or search engine advertising in order to appear at the top of search engine rankings. The down side of paying to be ranked is that such tactics cost money and some consumers are getting smarter, knowing that some sites are paying to be at the top. But the up side is that you are gaining exposure and hopefully making money. See my resource page for how to incorporate these tactics if you want to try them.

Must-Have Web Pages for Speakers

Eight pages every speaker must include in his or her web site:

1. **Home page.** Briefly explains who you are and what you do.

2. **Bio page.** Provides more in-depth information on who you are, and your background.

3. **Services page or Seminars/Keynotes/ Training page.** Describes your services.

4. **Testimonials page.** Rave reviews about you; this tells visitors who your clients have been and how great you are.

5. **Calendar of events.** People like to know what you are doing and when you are available.

6. **Newsletter.** Everyone needs one of these. It builds credibility, and adds to your contact list and client base.

7. **"Contact Us" page.** Here you put all your contact information. Include your name, telephone and fax number(s) and e-mail address. Add your street address if you choose.

8. **Meeting Planners and Bureaus page.** Here you link to all your marketing materials, like your speaking bio, headshots, introduction, testimonials,

video, pre-program questionnaire, reasons to hire you, etc.

Design

The first thing a new visitor to your web site judges you by is the look and feel of your web site. The way it works, how it looks, what the navigation is like and what words are used tell the visitor a lot about you before you have the opportunity to introduce yourself. Choose a look and feel that you are comfortable and confident with. Visit other web sites and make notes about what you like and do not like, for your web designer. Most of all, develop a professional look. It is important that your web site matches all of your marketing tools, including your business cards, brochures and promotional material.

How Much Should My Web Site Cost?

The cost of a good-looking web site can be anything from free to $10,000 and up. If you are on a shoestring budget I suggest partnering with a student looking to build a web design portfolio or someone who likes to do web site design on the side. I caution you that in some cases you get what you pay for. That said, be aware that people who charge big bucks often know a lot about how to make a web site flashy, but nothing about how to ensure your web site is search engine-friendly. Ask your colleagues and friends who they recommend.

Navigation

Navigation is critical to keep web site visitors at a web site. If a web site is hard to navigate, people will often get frustrated and leave—unless, of course, they really, really, really like the person who owns it and/or they are getting paid to browse.

Here are some tips for creating a navigation-friendly web site.

- Include a navigation bar on the left side of your web page or along the top.

- Create well-labelled navigation buttons.

- Make navigation easy enough for a five-year-old.

- Include a site map that tells people where to find items on your web site.

Getting Found on the Internet: Search Engines

Search engine dynamics change all the time. It is crucial to be at the top of search engine rankings so that people who are searching for you on the Internet can find you. In the old Internet days it was easy to be at the top of search engines, but now it can be a tireless full-time job to ensure your web site reaches the top.

This is the tricky part of dealing with the Internet. It changes as fast as people change their minds. Many people are advocating misleading or old techniques that no longer work. A few weeks ago I was speaking to someone who teaches web site and Internet marketing only to find out that he was giving out misinformation. Unfortunately, this is common. To be ranked at the top of a search engine, you have to know what the latest strategies are, and you must design your web site to be search engine-friendly right from the beginning.

Instead of filling this section with site submission techniques that may be outdated by the time you read this book, search engine specialist Jim Maddox has kindly agreed to share his free reports with you. You are invited to go to my resource page, look up "search engines" or "Jim Maddox" and click on the link, and Jim's free report will give you all the latest information about how to get top rankings. As the information changes I will update the resource page.

Internet Marketing

Internet marketing requires dedication, discipline and proper preparation and research. This topic could be a complete chapter—no, actually a book—on its own. If you want to incorporate Internet marketing into your online presence, hire an expert in the field, take a course or do some research. It is wise to ask around to find out who is the best at the moment. Terry Dean and Corey Rudl are two experts who currently have their fingers on the pulse of Internet marketing. What I like about Terry and Corey's services are the membership sites they have set up for people. The membership sites are kept up to date in real time. Everything is current. You are able to see live examples of people's successes and what they are doing well.

When you invest in an Internet marketing course, study the material, learn from it and, most importantly, APPLY it! Links to Internet marketing resources, free newsletters and products are on my resource page at **www.dare2feel.com/speakers.htm**.

If I had one piece of Internet marketing advice to give you on my own, it is to start an online newsletter or e-zine and get as many subscribers to it as you can. Take the time to build your newsletter list. It is worth every moment and every bit of energy you put into it. Your newsletter or e-zine helps you gain trust and build rapport, and it's where you'll get your business from in the long run. All Internet marketing experts will tell you this.

Your Gold Mine: E-Zines and Newsletters

Your e-zine (electronic magazine) or online newsletter is your number one marketing tool when it comes to the Internet. In this case, size does matter. The more people who receive your newsletter or e-zine, the more potential buyers you can build a relationship with and sell to.

The key to your e-zine list is to nurture it and grow it. It is ideal to have a clear target market in mind when you launch your e-zine.

Joel Christopher is a list-builder guru. His free e-zine informs and inspires people to build the email/newsletter/e-zine list of their dreams. You can access Joel's e-zine from my resource page under "How to Build Your E-Zine List". His information is hot and relevant.

What Are Auto-Responders?

An auto-responder is an e-mail delivered automatically to a client or customer. It is a brilliant

Internet follow-up and marketing tool. I use auto-responders three different ways.

1. When I am going to be out of the office for an extended period of time, I want people who send me an e-mail to know when I will be returning. If I get e-mail while I am away from the office an auto-responder is sent out immediately to the sender indicating when I will return and how to contact me.

2. Everyone who signs up to my e-zine *Zenergy News* receives an auto-responder containing "bonus" items for signing up. These are programmed to go out automatically. The auto-responders give me an opportunity to build a relationship with my new subscribers, which in turn builds trust, which turns them into paying customers.

3. All my e-courses and e-classes are delivered through auto-responders.

How Do Auto-Responders Work?

To use auto-responders you have to buy a monthly auto-responder service, own auto-responder software, or have auto-responders programmed into your web site.

Monthly services include companies such as **1shopingcart**, **getresponse** and **postmaster**. These companies are listed on my resource page under "E-Zine and Newsletter Tools". The investment for a monthly service ranges from $20 US a month to hundreds of dollars a month. You can get a good service for under $50.

The benefit of paying a monthly fee is that your auto-responders are run from an independent server. They are not hosted on your web site, or on your computer. This is important if you do not have the space to host all your newsletters, subscribers, and auto-responders on your computer. It is also good if you do not want the technical headaches of looking after everything yourself. Having said that, I should mention that it is very easy to run an auto-responder program from your business or home computer. I have coached many non-technical people to do so.

Personally, I own the **Postmaster** auto-responder software program and it handles all my auto-responder needs. I am very happy with the customer service and the software itself. Currently it starts at $199 US. **Mailloop** is a similar program.

The benefit of paying up front for me is that in the long term it keeps more money in my business. The biggest obstacle for most people is that you have to run the program from your own computer. I find this easy because I automate everything. Automation means I do not have to tend to each purchaser and newsletter/e-course subscriber individually. The software takes care of it all for me! If for some reason I have the automation turned off I send and receive e-mail once a day. This simple action takes care of sending and receiving all my auto-responder messages. It is simple and brilliant!

The final option is to have an auto-responder system programmed into the back end of your web site. This back end programming to send out multiple auto-responders can be costly, but I have simple one-time auto-responders programmed into my web site to instantly send out welcome letters to people when they sign up for a service or for *Zenergy News*. This is very affordable, and easy to do on most web sites.

Shop around for a combination that suits your needs.

Far Out Tools

Creating E-Courses, E-Classes and E-Books

I love e-courses, e-classes and e-books. Some of my most successful e-courses to date are *101 Healthy Habits*, *Seven Secrets to Balance*, and *Neck and Shoulder Daily Revitalizers*. E-courses and e-classes can be created about anything—from *How to Market Yourself on the Web* to *Customer Service Dos and Don'ts* to *Why Organic Food is Good*. They are fun to create, simple to implement and easy to facilitate once they are running. You can even add video and audio to make them more interactive.

The e-courses and e-classes I run do not need me to be an active participant in the class or course. When people sign up for an e-course they automatically receive a welcome letter in the sign-up window, and the auto-responder adds them to the e-course database. Once they are added to the database, the selected e-course knows to send out the class material on the scheduled days. I do nothing except make sure the e-class materials go out daily. I LOVE it! People get service from me while I leverage my time completing other activities. Creating automatic systems for our speaking business is a good thing because it allows us to leverage our time to do other things like marketing, personal customer service or finishing that book we've been meaning to write.

E-books are incredible tools for speakers. They add credibility, become another product to sell, and act as a promotional tool. If you have not written a book and want to, an e-book is a great place to begin. They can easily be sold or given away from your web site.

Adding Video and Audio

Video and audio tracks can be added to web sites easily. If you have more time than money it is simple to do it yourself. If you have more money than time, perhaps it is wiser to hire an expert.

Typically the best ways to post video and audio are in Real Media, Windows Media or QuickTime formats. Most people will have one or all of these programs on their computers. Be sure to format the audio and video files for people who are on telephone modems and for people who are on cable or DSL modems. File quality will be lower with the phone modem because it is slower, but the user will be able to watch and listen.

If you decide to edit and program the files yourself, Adobe Premiere is a great program to use. To create Real files you will need software from **Real.com**. Learn how to add video or audio to your web site by visiting my resource page for more information.

Selling Product Online

Security Issues

Many speakers have books, CDs, audio tapes or other products available. A natural extension of back-of-the-room product sales is selling such products online from your web site.

The biggest obstacle preventing people from buying something online is that they fear their credit card or personal information will be stolen, used or sold. To counteract this fear it is important to make the buyer feel safe. The first way to do that is to make sure your sales occur through a secure (encrypted) web server. A secure server not only makes it easy to accept online payment, it also protects the consumer's personal and confidential information. See the following section for more information about secure servers and online payment methods.

Other ways to make your buyers feel safe are:

- Build trust with buyers by telling them their information is confidential and that they are on a secure Internet page for purchasing.

- Openly display your picture, address, e-mail, phone number and contact information on your web site

- Tell the buyer their information will never be sold or shared

- Remind buyers that they are purchasing from a secure web server. Point out the lock icon at the bottom of the browser window, which they should be able to see. This indicates that all information moving back and forth is encrypted (coded) and thus safe.

Taking Payment

To sell products online you can either use a third-party billing service or obtain your own e-commerce gateway and merchant account.

Third-party billing companies include **PayPal**, **IBill** and **QuickPayPro**. I have not used any of these services, but I know others who do and they are very happy. These companies will typically keep a percentage of your sales in exchange for providing you with the ability to accept credit cards online. All credit card transactions go through the third party's secure gateway server.

When you have your own online merchant account and e-merchant gateway all transactions go through your own business gateway. This is more costly up front, but if you have a lot of revenue from product sales then it is well worth the investment.

In my experience it is best to start with a third-party billing system until you have enough online business to warrant your own gateway. When you obtain your own gateway and merchant account you will need to get a Thawte Security Certificate that certifies your credit card processing as secure. Some hosting and e-commerce companies will let you use theirs. In my opinion, the best Canadian company for setting up your own gateway is **PsiGate.com**. I have been very happy with their services.

Go For It!

I encourage you to incorporate the Internet and technology into your speaking business. It has leveraged my business significantly. Remember to design a web site you like that makes you money. Be Web-wise in your decisionmaking.

I hope you found some value in this chapter and some tools that will take your speaking career to greater heights.

Natalie Forstbauer
Dr. Feel Good
P: 604-737-3632
Toll free 877-559-3273
F: 760-462-2910
natalie@dare2feel.com
www.dare2feel.com

About Natalie Forstbauer

Natalie's Internet savvy was born from her desire to leverage her time through technology. Her speaking business web site is host to a variety of technical bells and whistles that are search engine-friendly, user-friendly and business-friendly. They include a password-protected, automated health membership portal called

Zenergy, an electronic e-zine, complete business automation, web forms for clients to fill out, search engine-friendly web pages, the use of Internet marketing tools, auto-responders, streaming video and streaming audio clips, e-commerce technologies, and more. Visit her speakers' resource page to learn how to leverage your speaking business with technology and the Internet: **www.dare2feel.com/speakers.htm** .

Whether speaking to a large audience or chatting over coffee, Natalie motivates people in a positive way. She lives up to her pseudonym "Dr. Feel Good". An author and syndicated columnist, she is the president of **dare2feel Training & Development International**.

Natalie is an expert in healthy living and life balance. In her keynotes and seminars she reveals instant, usable and doable solutions that allow you to get a handle on your health when you have no time. Her book *Health in a Hurry: Simple Solutions for the Time-Starved* (dare2feel, 2004) discloses Natalie's secrets to being healthy in a time-starved world.

Natalie's goal is to touch people's lives in a positive way worldwide. Through her humour, charisma, and enchanting personality people find the wealth of joy and love she shares contagious.

You're Speaking—But Are You Connecting? Developing Your Stories

by Margaret Hope, M.Ed.

The Power of Stories

Imagine yourself standing on a low stage with a hot, tired audience struggling desperately to remain attentive. It's early in your career and you are trying just as desperately to impress the host group. You have enough experience to know with absolute certainty that your efforts are failing. Then imagine yourself plunging through the stage. While disappearing might be exactly what you wished for, even this wish is denied. Only your foot went through. It wedged there and now you are trapped in the stage.

When this actually happened to me, I received two valuable gifts: I learned that bored, miserable audiences love it when the speaker has an on-stage disaster. I also acquired a story that has been useful ever since. I often use it to help speakers understand how an on-stage disaster can help them forge a bond—connect—with audiences.

As listeners, stories have the most wonderful power to transport us to a moment. They can help us feel what the storyteller felt, remember key points from a speech and entertain us. They provide respite from serious content.

As speakers, stories help us create chemistry with our audiences—to connect with us on an emotional level. Connecting emotionally is what enhances memory and facilitates understanding.

Long before humans had a written language, they understood the power of stories. Ancient cultures universally chose stories as a way to ensure their history and beliefs were passed along to future generations. Storytellers travelled from place to place, well-rewarded for the entertainment and education they provided. Today, professional speakers are appreciated for the same reasons and in much the same way. But we can't do it without our stories.

Tell Your Stories, Not Mine

I fell through the stage in Barbados in 1985, so that story is mine. As a professional speaker you will have your own collection of stories. The best will be drawn from your life. Since you've lived them you'll be able to tell them with the energy, colour and emotion that no one else could ever hope to equal. You are your own best source of material.

Stories are everywhere, but that doesn't mean you can or should use every one you hear. Don't claim stories as your own if they didn't happen to you. If you hear a speaker use a story, ask permission if you want to use it and credit that individual with the material—not once, but every time you use it. If the story happened to someone else, tell it as his or her story. If the story is in wide circulation, such as the many stories dispersed by e-mail or those published in widely read journals such as *Reader's Digest*, avoid using it.

As powerful as a story may be, no audience should have to hear the same one twice in one day. A colleague of mine once arrived to deliver a luncheon plenary. The keynote speaker earlier in the day had opened with the very story she had planned to use in her closing. She described the cold panic she felt when she heard of the duplication. She told me how she scrambled to revamp her speech with only moments to go before the master of ceremonies introduced her. That near-miss experience was the catalyst to start preparing and using her own material. My colleague has now had such success relating her own life experiences to audiences that she wonders why she ever used generic material.

Collect Your Stories

Make it a practice to write out the events of your life, small or large. You can archive them as mindmaps, as journal entries, on file cards or in your computer. Ideally you'd have the perfect filing system so you could instantly retrieve a sublime specimen, but having lived them and recorded them, although you might not find the precise entry, you'll probably remember most of your stories when you need them. Even if you have no use for a story today, you may eventually find it useful to illustrate a key point, raise an issue or engender an emotional state in your audience.

Go beyond your own immediate recollection. A newspaper article can help you create a story by triggering memories of long-forgotten experiences and helping you tap into strong feelings.

I once read an article about an impoverished young mother raising three children in a dank basement suite while trying to improve her lot by attending college. She'd left her family and close-knit rural community in a determined effort to upgrade her education and secure a better life for her family, but the immediate future looked dim. It was December 24, and while her children excitedly discussed Santa's imminent arrival, she faced a sad reality. There would be no tree, no gifts, no turkey dinner and no festive celebration. Her heart ached for her sweet children. She was alone and incapable of providing. She'd heard there were agencies that would help but she thought they were for the truly needy and would not—perhaps, could not—admit that she needed the help. She had hoped for a small parcel from her grandmother or a friend but there was no delivery, and as the afternoon faded so did her hope. Finally she knew she had to help her small children understand that Santa would not appear.

Just as she began to speak, there was a loud noise at her door. Not a knock, not a tap, more of a muffled thump, as if an entire human body had collided with the door. Tremulously she opened the door just enough to see out. And there, under the bare bulb that lit her stoop, she found three smiling teenagers. One carried a decorated tree, another carried two bulging bags of groceries and a third bore colourfully wrapped parcels. Somewhere someone else knew of her situation and made the call that brought Christmas to her home. She was not alone.

I'm not sure what that story means to you. As I read it, it brought back memories of childhood and family celebrations. I thought of times when I felt inadequate or hopeless, times when I was too proud to ask for help and times when someone else reached out to let me know I was not alone. Each of those memories stimulated stories. And some of those stories became valuable parts of my speeches and presentations. Writing to capture the feelings in your stories is a powerful tool for creating new anecdotal material.

Don't limit yourself to the newspaper when seeking inspiration. A friend or family member might offer you a story, biographies and autobiographies can provide stories of notable heroes, or your volunteer work might contribute a story about an unsung hero. In fact, if you read widely and listen carefully, stories are everywhere.

Now Craft Your Stories

I've already recommended that you keep a diary or collection of your personal experiences. Don't imagine that they will be useful just as they happened. You'll need to edit them into useful pieces. Here are the concerns I address when crafting stories.

Purpose: Before selecting a story, ask yourself, "What point am I trying to make?" Also ask yourself, "What feeling do I want my listeners to experience?" These simple questions will lead you to the best stories in your personal collection.

Cast: Limit your cast of characters—the fewer the better. Develop each character with only the essential elements. Their emotions and responses are frequently more important than details of how you know them, their marital state, careers, ages and physical attributes.

Plot: Edit the plot to include only the essentials. Your story needs a setting. Then it needs to move through a period of tension, build to a climax, release and make a point. Lengthy stories work well when the speech is primarily for entertainment, inspiration or motivation (e.g., a keynote or plenary). Such stories often have sub-climaxes that build to the main point. For training presentations, stories are often shorter to ensure the audience doesn't lose the point being illustrated.

Details: Paint vivid details that help listeners experience the story as if we were part of it. *"A prickling sensation rippled across her back and settled heavily at her throat"* will do more to transport the audience than *"She was afraid"*. *"He climbed purposefully upwards through sharp rocks, lichens and scree"* will paint a stronger picture than *"He hiked above the treeline"*.

Limits: Despite the suggestion above, it isn't wise to swallow a thesaurus or assault your audience with endless details. Simply provide enough colour to engage them and help them climb inside the story with you. If you re-read the story about the family in crisis at Christmas, you'll notice you have no idea of the age of the children or the mother, yet you likely had a vision of their impoverished existence and their feelings.

Climax: Consider the climax of your story. This is like the punchline of a joke. You build to it, you pause, you wait for the audience to indicate its readiness and then you deliver it. You pause again to let the emotional release occur. Then, while the audience is attentive, you deliver your point—the point you planned to make when you identified your purpose and chose the story.

Refine the Truth

Kenneth McFarland, a renowned American speaker, often said, "It's a poor public speaker who can't tell a story better than it happened." I don't mean to encourage you to invent a glorious fictitious past for yourself. (I've been with speakers who appear to have done precisely that. I didn't enjoy their blatant puffery.) I do encourage you to prepare your material so it has maximum impact on your listener. As you become focused on achieving a specific outcome with a story, certain aspects of that story will need to be emphasized and other aspects omitted or under-played. I think it is acceptable and necessary to edit your version of the story, even if that isn't as accurate as a longer account would be.

There will even be times when your story is clearly an invention. I have a story about two ants on a golf course. Since the ants have a discussion about their survival, I'm pretty sure the average listener knows the story is a fabrication. I don't think audiences regard this as dishonest any more than they'd think folk tales, fairy tales and Aesop's fables are dishonest.

It is more important to have a story that is effective than one that is meticulously accurate. Crafting and refining your story is not simply about writing or planning. It is as much about how you deliver it as it is about the content itself. That means you need to spend time rehearsing your material.

Rehearse

The best speakers I've ever heard tell me they still rehearse their stories. And not just the new material they are incorporating—they also rehearse their mature material.

Whether new or old, each story is like an unframed work of art. By selecting a certain mat and frame, you highlight specific details in the artwork. Likewise voice, body language, timing, and props all serve to draw out specific elements in the story. By rehearsing aloud you can focus on reducing the story to its essential components and begin to give emphasis to critical aspects of the story. When rehearsing your stories:

Improve the sound. Refine your voice and vocabulary by recording the story. Although you can use a tape recorder, most telephone voice mail systems work well for this. Experiment with longer pauses and try varying the volume, pitch, pace, and tone. As you listen to the replay, notice repetitive word choices and intonation patterns, since these can drain all the life from an otherwise good story.

Add physical excitement. Hone your physical delivery in front of a large window. If the room is brightly illuminated and it's dark outside, you'll instantly see and be able to correct the physical aspects of your delivery. Because it offers a large viewing area, you can move as you will when you tell the story before a live audience. You'll also want to work on pausing, changing your posture, shifting your weight, tilting your head and generally becoming more dramatic. This is also the right place to experiment with simple props, costume items or visual aids.

Use your face. Mirrors are perfect for rehearsing facial expression, which, especially during your powerful pauses, adds much to the impact on the audience. Your look of rapt concern as you pause just before the punchline strengthens the tension of the moment.

Star in your own movie. Video can be used to evaluate most aspects of your delivery although it does not offer the immediate feedback of a window or mirror. One of the best ways to use it is with a speech coach or evaluator.

Get feedback. Once you're reasonably satisfied with the story, begin to tell it to your speech coach, friends, colleagues and family. Watch their reactions for signs of boredom or confusion. Also notice when they laugh, or when they appear spellbound or emotionally involved. Ask for specific feedback on the overall effect, rather than on a specific skill like your use of pauses or eye contact. The goal is to achieve a certain outcome with the story, not to have perfect delivery.

Finally, work the story into a speech and watch the audience each time you deliver it. When the story begins to feel cumbersome or isn't getting the reaction it once did, either retire it or take it back to its essential components and rehearse it until it is powerful again.

Play with Your Audience

While I don't think of audience interaction as a skill for beginners, I do admire the many skilled speakers who invite the audience to participate in their stories. Jeff Mowatt, past national president of the Canadian Association of Professional Speakers, is a great example. When he addressed our Vancouver chapter some years ago, Jeff told part of a story about a young boy. At a critical moment he paused, asked us to turn to our immediate neighbour and think of words to describe how the child might have been feeling at that moment. We buzzed, he asked for responses, many were offered and he went on with the story—incorporating our ideas. I believe this interaction engaged us in his very personal story. Interaction is a way to intensify audience response.

I tell a story about having to rescue my father and bring him home from Arizona. After explaining why a commercial plane couldn't be used, I tell about canvassing our many friends and business acquaintances: "To my amazement, one of our friends offered us the use of his private jet." This provides a perfect moment for inter-action. I ask if any of my audience happens to have a jet parked in the backyard. I point out the rather obvious fact that I'm not the kind of person who expects friends to have such a thing. Occasionally someone in the audience knows someone with a private or corporate jet—which allows me to point out that I'm not the only one with surprisingly wealthy friends. We laugh and move on to the rest of the rescue story. That brief interaction provides momentary respite in a fairly lengthy story. It also allows me to reinforce the theme of the story, which is that we all have a multitude of resources available to us through our personal networks.

While we generally think of storytelling as simply relating a tale, it can go far beyond that by engaging the listener and strengthening the connection between speaker and listener. As your confidence builds, become creative in how you tell stories and how you invite the audience to participate.

Don't Give Up

Whether you create purely fictitious stories (ants who talk, or children who loudly proclaim the nakedness of pompous emperors), tell stories of those who have inspired you (Helen Keller still inspires me), edit stories from your own amazing life, involve the audience in your stories or simply relate the facts, those stories will enrich your speeches and win you the adoration of your audiences. Great storytellers practice their material every chance they get. They are constantly observing audience response and revising their stories based on those observations.

Storytelling is not particularly easy, but it is within your reach.

Margaret F. Hope, M.Ed.
Lionsgate Training Ltd.
4649 Hastings St.
Burnaby, BC V5C 2K6
P: 604-320-7613
F: 604-320-1660
mhope@lionsgatetraining.com
www.lionsgatetraining.com

About Margaret Hope

Clients have described Margaret Hope as "totally professional," "refreshingly practical" and "ever-so-slightly irreverent." They're talking about the custom-designed keynotes, conference programs and communications training she provides for a wide variety of business clients on four continents.

Margaret Hope, president of **Lionsgate Training Ltd.**, holds a master's degree in (speech) education and is an Accredited Professional Speaker—only fifty-two speakers worldwide have received this performance-based accreditation. She is the author of *You're Speaking—But Are You Connecting?* (LGTL, 1998), and is a contributing author to *Strategies for Engineering Communication* (Wiley, 2002). She is an adjunct professor at Simon Fraser University and an instructor at the University of BC. In addition to the training and speaking mentioned above, she also provides speech coaching for executive clients and aspiring professional speakers.

Margaret balances her life with volunteer work and family. She is a Paul Harris Fellow of Rotary International and a past International Director of Toastmasters International. She hikes, kayaks near her home in the Gulf Islands and is the only Canadian woman to operate her own railway speeder.

And One More Thing...

Everyone Loves a Great Story!

by Abegael Fisher-Lang

It's not just a catchy CAPS maxim that the power of speaking can transform the world. It's been known since ancient times. And the simplest form of speaking is storytelling. A folk art as old as the hills, and yet an agent for profound transformation, storytelling leads us back to the core of human experience, and teaches us how to simply speak, and to speak simply. That's why all world cultures recognize the opening of a story-space with invocations such as "Cric? Crac!" or "Once upon a time..." Such invocations let people know, "Ah! Now the speaking will be different than before, the listening will be different... We are in a new place."

Storytelling opens a no-stress listening space that, curiously, facilitates greater learning even though it appears that the listener is simply enjoying and responding to a story. The way in which material is presented communicates more than the actual spoken word because storytelling, and indeed all speaking, is a performance medium. The transformative power of a story arises from a meeting of imaginations, and relies on the inner preparation of the teller. But oddly, although people remember only 8 to10 percent of content from a presentation, speakers spend most of their preparation time on content rather than delivery.

An enlivened delivery is essential to good speaking, and it is the key to great storytelling. In the critical first minute of presenting, before any content has been conveyed, a storyteller engages an audience immediately on a human level. Avoiding the usual humdrum introduction, she takes a creative risk and opens with a surprise: a metaphor, an anecdote, a dramatic statement, a poem or a song. Leading with her imagination, she inspires listeners to call upon their own powers of imagination.

Her enthusiasm is as compelling as her mastery of expressive language. Having learned her material almost by heart, she does not read from notes (or worse, her Powerpoint slides). She maintains eye contact. If something unexpected happens, she has the flexibility and the skill to let go of her prepared format altogether and change direction.

She readily tells stories of her own challenges and struggles. Though she is always looking for new story material, she has a repertoire of lively and well-formed stories that adapt to a variety of situations.

When asked, she will say that her commitment is to enliven her listeners, not merely to convey information. Continually inspired by the mysterious activity of storytelling she experiences storytelling as a process that transforms. Not surprisingly, so do her listeners!

The difference between speaking and storytelling, in a nutshell, is the power of imagination. It is through "inviting the muse" that a story can transform teller and listener. A wise speaker never memorizes a text, but strives to experience the story through an imaginative rather than a cognitive process. Rendering a story through a series of creative movement and visualization exercises ensures that the teller's imagination is engaged, and, as if by magic, so is the imagination of every listener.

Often the courage to use stories is what distinguishes a great speaker from a good speaker. There is a place in presentation work for all kinds of stories—for instance, folk tales are in the public domain, and can be freely adapted and retold.

Great speakers know that personal stories can be golden threads in a successful presentation. A personal story can be extremely powerful, though it's a challenge to be objective in shaping it for maximum impact. Hint: simplify, simplify, simplify! Be sure all details you include are essential to the main point of the story. Remember, another speaker's personal stories are solely for his or her use, including personal adaptations of folk tales. As Joseph Campbell often commented, "Every story you tell is your own story."

Rational thinking takes us from A to B, mused Albert Einstein, but imagination takes us everywhere. Storytelling takes a wild ride on imagination's flying carpet with the stories of all time woven through it. The silver threads are the world tales we all share, but the golden threads are your unique life stories.

Come on. Tell a great story!

Abegael Fisher-Lang
Mythopoetica Storytelling
Box 16206 Lynn Valley PO
North Vancouver, BC V7J 3S9
P: 604-985-5168
afl@mythopoetica.ca
www.mythopoetica.ca

About Abegael Fisher-Lang

An acclaimed storyteller and educator, Abegael Fisher-Lang invites the muse regularly! As the owner of **Mythopoetica Storytelling** she presents story-based workshops for organizations, coaches the dynamics of storytelling, and creates story curricula with the international program *Learning Through the Arts*™. She facilitates creative story events such as the Welsh Mabinogion Epic 2003, and will be profiled in the West Vancouver Community Arts Council's new book *Mentors in our Midst* for her work in developing community storytelling. With skill and humour, she inspires her colleagues to invite the muse in these workshops for speakers: *Tell a Great Story* and *Following the Thread: Personal Stories, Sacred Stories*. Details of upcoming workshops and events can be gleaned from her web site at **www.mythopoetica.ca** .

How to Captivate Your Audience with Stand-Up Comedy

by David Granirer, MA

Why Stand-Up Comedy?

If you've hung out at CAPS or NSA you've probably heard this saying: Do you need to use humour in your presentations? Only if you want to get paid! Well, it's true. One big difference between high-level keynoters and entry-level speakers is the number of laughs they get. As a matter of fact, I've seen highly paid keynote speakers whose content boils down to platitudes like "teamwork is good," "be the best you can be," and "take a positive attitude to life." Despite this lack of content, these speakers receive rave reviews! When I've asked attendees what they liked about these presentations, the answer is always something like, "He/she was so funny, so entertaining, so hilarious."

That's right, folks. We're not only in the business of educating people. We're also in the business of entertaining them. Our job is to make them laugh, and perhaps to slip in a few easily-digested and non-controversial bits of content. I'm not saying this is good or bad, but as far as I can tell it's the reality of our business. The more laughs we get, the more we can charge.

And that's where stand-up comedy comes in. One of the most important goals of stand-up comedy is to get as many laughs per minute (LPMs) as you can. The idea is that the setup to a joke (the part that comes before the laugh) is as short as possible so you can maximize your LPMs. And the great thing about having stand-up comedy material is that you can go through your presentation and decide exactly how many laughs you want at any given point.

What Stand-Up Comedy Is and Isn't

Stand-up comedy is about 80 percent written and rehearsed, with 20 percent ad-libbed. And even that 20 percent of so-called ad-libbed material includes many prepared lines. In stand-up comedy, preparation is the key. You leave very little to chance.

Stand-up comedy is not about telling the funny stories that crack up your friends. Getting laughs from an audience of strangers is totally different. Your friends know you and understand exactly where you're coming from. So you can tell a funny story about your uncle Ed, building up to the climax, "Then Uncle Ed made this weird face..." and they'll all laugh because they know Uncle Ed and his idiosyncrasies. Unfortunately, an audience of strangers doesn't know and doesn't care who Uncle Ed is, so when you get to the funny part about him making a face they'll just sit there in dead silence. I can't begin to count the number of times students have come into my comedy course figuring it'll be a breeze because all they have to do is tell funny stories. Usually they have to die a few times before they get it.

Another problem with stories is that they can take too long to get to the punchline. Comedy is about tension and release. As you set up a joke, tension rises because the audience is waiting for a payoff in the form of a laugh. The longer it takes you to get to the laugh, the greater the tension becomes and the bigger the expectations are that what you're saying is going to be hilarious. So if you take three minutes to get to the funny part, people expect a huge laugh. In other words, you've set yourself up for a big fall. That's why in stand-up comedy there's never more than about thirty seconds between setup and punchline.

Don't Steal

Stand-up comedy is also not about taking a funny bit you've heard a comic use and pretending it's your own. Jokes are intellectual property. Whoever wrote them probably spent a lot of time on each joke. Also, you're bound to get caught. Sooner or later someone in your audience will recognize that Dennis Miller bit you've passed off as your own. You'll damage your reputation among other speakers, and any comics that find out will hate you forever.

This also applies to taking someone's joke, changing a few words and then pretending it's your own, or trying to pass off a joke you've heard at a party as your own. All it does is lessen the value of your presentation. Lots of people in your audience can get up and tell jokes they've heard at parties or on TV, so why should they pay you to do it?

Now, to be fair, there are a lot of people out there writing jokes, so there is a chance that you may write a joke that's similar to someone else's. In this case it's okay, because it's an honest coincidence. A friend of mine faxes jokes to Jay Leno. They told him not to freak out if he hears a joke very similar to one he wrote make it on to the show, because Leno has thousands of people faxing in topical bits every day, and there's a good chance people will take similar angles.

The Basic Formula

Here is the basic formula for writing stand-up comedy. In general, humour involves exaggeration and/or surprise. For something to be funny there must be some sort of surprise twist and/or exaggeration of reality. If the punchline is predictable, no one will laugh.

Jokes consist of a setup and a punchline, or multiple punchlines. The setup is not meant to be funny. It often consists of a fact or opinion, like: *People often say to me, "David, you're brave to do stand-up comedy."* A good setup is also short and to the point, no longer than fifteen or twenty seconds, and contains no more than one idea. Often a setup will include your attitude: how you feel about what you're talking about. Do you hate it? Love it? Does it scare you? Often what's funny is not your topic, but your attitude towards it.

The punchline is the funny part of a joke. It stands in contrast to the setup and contains an unexpected twist or exaggeration. The setup creates certain expectations, which the punchline then shatters.

Here's an example of a complete joke. I've taken the fact I gave you earlier and used it as a setup. People often say to me, *"David, you're brave to do stand-up comedy."* This fact creates certain logical expectations. For example, we'd expect that the people who say it to me are audience members and that they say it at my comedy shows. To shatter this expectation I have to substitute something different from what people are expecting. In other words, other than audience members at my shows, who else and where else would people say, "David, you're brave to do stand-up comedy?" My substitution is that instead of audience members, the people saying this are my counseling clients, and that they're saying it to me during our sessions. Thus the entire joke looks like this:

Setup: People often say to me, "David, you're brave to do stand-up comedy."

Punchline: But they only say it when I'm counseling them.

Here's another example. Let's take this fact: *As a counselor, I meet some really bitter, angry, sick people.* Obviously, we expect those people to be my clients. In my substitution I need to figure out who else these bitter, angry, sick people are. My answer is "my colleagues". Here's the entire joke.

Setup: As a counselor, I meet some really bitter, angry, sick people.

Punchline: And those are just the other counselors.

Make sure you put the punch word, the word that triggers the laugh, last. You'll notice that the last word in this joke is *counselors*. The punchline would be much less effective if it was, *And the counselors I work with are the people I'm talking about.* People will start to laugh when they hear the word "counselor," and if I continue on after that, they will quickly stop laughing to hear what else I have to say.

Generating Material

People often say that their humour is spontaneous, so a structured process for generating humour feels too contrived. And spontaneous humour is great! Unfortunately it doesn't always happen. Think of the structured process I'm about to show you as a form of "prepared spontaneity." You prepare so well that your humour sounds spontaneous to your audience.

Probably the worst place to start when you're writing humour about something is to ask yourself, "How do I make this funny?" "Funny" is a vague, nebulous term that provides no structure to the writing process, and the better your structure, the better your chances for success. Here, then, is a five-step structured process for generating comedy material:

1. Choose something you'd like to write about. This something could be a topic you present, a story you'd like to tell, or almost anything else.

2. Write down ten facts about your chosen subject. If you want to tell a story, then each development in your story becomes a separate fact. For example, if you're talking about your family reunion, Fact #1 could be: *I flew home on Alaska Airlines.* Fact #2 could be: *My brother picked me up at the airport,* and so on. Remember, you're not trying to be funny at this point. All you want are the facts and just the facts. For example, let's say my topic was smoking. Some facts about smoking are:

- My doctor says that smoking causes cancer.

- I get sick when someone smokes while I'm eating.

- I'm glad they've banned smoking in restaurants.

The facts from Step Two are now my setups. One by one I take my setups and look for expectations to shatter. Please note that by "expectations" I'm referring to expectations that would logically arise from a given statement, not something bizarre or off-the-wall. At this point I'm not trying to be funny. I'm saving that for the punchline. For example:

Setup: My doctor says that smoking causes cancer. What expectations do I have when I hear the above statement? I'd expect that:

- My doctor doesn't smoke.

- He/she wants me to quit.

- My doctor says it to me.

- He/she says it during my appointments.
- Smoking refers to smoking cigarettes.

Now I choose one of my expectations and come up with a substitution. Let's say I chose expectation #5, that smoking refers to smoking cigarettes. To get a punchline I'd ask myself, "What else could smoking refer to?"
For example:
- Smoking could refer to someone lighting you on fire.
- Smoking could refer to getting really mad.
- Smoking could refer to smoking drugs.

Now I choose one of my substitutions and make it into my punchline. I usually come up with three to five punchlines and choose the best. For example, let's say I choose substitution #3, that smoking refers to smoking drugs.
Setup: My doctor says that smoking causes cancer.
Sample punchlines:
- But that's no reason to shut down my grow-op.
- So now I only smoke cigarettes made from crack.
- But he mellowed out after I offered him a quarter-ounce.
- So now when I'm with friends I only inhale half the joint.

For my complete joke I'd choose punchline #3 because I think it's the best.
Setup: My doctor says that smoking causes cancer.

Punchline: But he mellowed out after I offered him a quarter-ounce.

Here is a quick encapsulation of the entire process.

Step One: Choose something you'd like to write about.

Step Two: Write down ten facts about your chosen subject.

Step Three: The facts from Step Two are now your setups. Take these setups and look for expectations to shatter.

Step Four: Choose one of your expectations and come up with a substitution.

Step Five: Choose one of your substitutions and make it into your punchline.

The Simpler the Better

When I outline this process people often say something like, "This sure is a lot of work." To which I respond, "Of course." Generating humour is a lot of work. As a matter of fact, I think it's the hardest kind of writing there is. And one of the hardest things about it is the simplicity of the process. It goes against everything we've been taught about writing.

When you're writing an essay or a speech, you must go into great detail to back up your opinions. Writing comedy is just the opposite. You leave out all the detail, keeping the bare minimum number of words you need to be coherent. Ruthlessly edit out anything that doesn't move the joke forward. I've heard it said that Jerry Seinfeld will spend an hour and a half to get a setup down from nine words to seven. Here's what I mean. Take the smoking joke from the previous section:

Setup: My doctor says that smoking causes cancer.

Punchline: But he mellowed out after I offered him a quarter-ounce.

Originally the fact I used for the setup was, *The other day I went in for my annual checkup. The doctor asked me if I smoked and I said, "No." He said, "Good, because you know smoking causes cancer."* But most of the words do nothing to move the joke forward, so I cut them out.

Road Testing Your Material

Once you've written a joke, the next step is to test it. This is crucial, because the bit about the mutant talking carrot that seemed hilarious at the time may not translate into anyone else's idea of what's funny. It's easy to lose perspective or have your ego get too attached to something you've just written.

That said, you need to give your jokes a chance. I always try a joke two or three times before I abandon it. Some of my best jokes bombed the first time around, and some jokes that killed the audience the first time never got a laugh after that. Some jokes I thought were hilarious bombed, whereas others I thought were poor ended up with a huge response.

Another way to give your new joke a fair shot is to position it in a good spot in your presentation. In general, I won't open with a new joke, because the audience usually isn't warmed up enough for me to get a proper reading of their response. I also won't place a new joke right after a sad or poignant story, for obvious reasons. My favourite place to put a new joke is after some light content at about the halfway mark of the presentation, once I've won the audience over.

A good joke should work about 90 percent of the time. A good success rate for writing jokes is about 30 percent (that is, 30 percent of the jokes you write will be funny), so you need volume in order to build a body of good material. I'd estimate that if I gathered all the material I've ever written, I'd have about four hours of comedy but only an hour would be funny. So don't get discouraged. Writing good material takes time, and lots of trial and error.

I often see ads for presentation skills seminars that promise quick, easy-to-learn techniques that will instantly turbo-charge your presentations and make you the toast of the speaking business. To which I want to reply, "If becoming a great speaker is that easy, then why should I pay to take your seminar? I can just figure it out for myself." In contrast, I can promise you that learning the art of stand-up comedy will take lots of time and effort. To really get it, you have to be persistent, determined, and prepared for the occasional bomb.

David Granirer, MA, RPC
Psychocomic.com Presentations Inc.
3633 Triumph St.
Vancouver, BC V5K 1V4
P: 604-205-9242
F: 604-205-9243
david@psychocomic.com
www.psychocomic.com

About David Granirer, MA, RPC

In addition to presenting keynotes and workshops, performing stand-up comedy, and serving as a psychotherapist in private practice, David Granirer teaches the stand-up comedy clinic at Langara College in Vancouver. In the past eight years he has turned hundreds of people with no experience and lots of desire into stand-up comics. Graduates of his course have performed at comedy festivals and on TV across Canada.

He also coaches speakers on how to use humour in their presentations, teaching them to maximize their number of laughs per minute. He has presented *How to Captivate Your Audience with Stand-Up Comedy* at CAPS and NSA conventions.

He has taught stand-up comedy clinics to mental health consumers, recovering drug addicts and cancer patients, helping them use humour to cope with their challenges. At the end of the course all students perform their material at a showcase in front of a live audience. One of his students says, "David's course is the best therapy I've ever had. By taking David's course, I went from VICTIM to VICTOR in only eight weeks!"

David also gives "laughter in the workplace" presentations to hundreds of organizations across North America, helping them use humour to reduce stress, increase wellness and cope with change.

His work is featured in newspapers and magazines, and on radio and TV throughout the US and Canada. He is also the author of the forthcoming book, *I'm OK But YOU Need Professional Help: How Being Neurotic and Fear-Driven Can Lead to Happiness And Success.* For more information, or to read his free articles on humour, go to **http://www.psychocomic.com** or call (604) 205-9242.

Speaking on the Funny Side of the Brain

by Carla Rieger

Picture this: I enter a seminar room filled with seventy hostile supervisors. None of them wants to be there. I have been hired to present on the topic *How to Lead Group Meetings*.

Their boss introduces me. There is no applause as I step up to the platform. I stand for a moment in silence as I study crossed arms and downturned faces. I say, "I'm here today to teach you *The Seven Most Successful Strategies for Skipping Out of Seminars*, and you obviously need help in this area."

Some light laughter. A number of arms uncross. Several faces look up. I list such topics as *How to Fake a Note from Your Doctor*, *Self-Cloning Made Easy* and *Whine Your Way to the Golf Course*. People are sitting up straight now instead of slouching in their seats. Their boss looks nervous, but I have her permission to use this approach.

The laughter softens people up enough for the next step. They choose partners and tell each other what they would rather be doing. More smiles, more faces light up. I then open the floor to discuss what is important to them. Many say they need to learn how to deal with difficult employees, not lead group meetings. Since that is part of the seminar anyway, I start with that topic. They seem much more open and willing now. Ironically, a participant asks, "How do you get a group of grumpy, unwilling people to participate?" All I have to do is stand there with a wry smile on my face and the whole room bursts into laughter.

The rest of the seminar is productive, creative and eye-opening. The boss is relieved. I thank her for trusting me. This is just one example of how humour enhances, and in some cases saves, a speaker's presentation.

Notice I say "humour" and not "comedy", because the two are different. I never considered myself a comedian. I was rarely the person telling the latest joke, doing pratfalls, or playing tricks on people. But I did notice that when people laughed, it was because I told a story or made an ironic observation. My early attempts at humour on the platform failed because I thought jokes were the only way to lighten up a group. The truth is, I neither had the talent, time or patience to write a good joke. By honing my innate humour skills first, I eventually built enough confidence to get groups laughing. After many years of researching a variety of humour forms and working with dozens of speakers, I created a humour personality profile.

Far too often I hear my clients say, "I'm just not funny!" Usually they are trying to be someone else. I believe everyone (given the right circumstances) can make people laugh if they start where they feel comfortable.

I worked with an IT manager whose boss promoted him to sales. His rival was what I call a *Demonstrator* humorist. She was lively and extroverted, and captivated her listeners with impressions and playing off her audience. My client felt extremely intimated by this style. Yet during our coaching sessions he often made witty observations on the sales process or hilarious self-deprecating remarks. He was more of a *Contemplator* humorist. I encouraged him to make note of his remarks and use them during his sales talks. As it turned out, even though his style was more low-key than his colleague's, he won people over with his humility and by remaining true to his own personality.

I also worked with an aspiring keynote speaker who thought she had to be a great story-teller like the Narrator speaker Jack Canfield. Yet she found it challenging to understand story structure and deliver anecdotes with animation. She had a very logical mind and liked to play with words. I suggested joke writing to her. She got Judy Carter's book *The Comedy Bible* (Fireside, 2001) and worked up a short stand-up act that successfully delivered her material in a light-hearted way.

There are five basic humour styles. Use your intuition to see where your strengths lie.

Demonstrators tend to be open, people-oriented, animated, and impetuous. The comedians

Robin Williams, Lucille Ball, Jim Carrey, and Carol Burnett all fit this profile. They are good at improvisation, caricatures, impressions, and physical comedy. A good way to enhance these skills is through comedy improvisation classes.

Narrators are warm and people-oriented, but more indirect and diplomatic. Bill Cosby, Mary Tyler Moore, and Johnny Carson fit this profile. Their type of humour is derived from relationships between people. They make good storytellers and do well using audience participation to elicit laughter. Try working through a book such as *A Story is a Promise* by Bill Johnson (Blue Heron, 2000).

Assertors are natural leaders, task-oriented and direct. The humorists David Letterman, John Cleese, Candice Bergen, and Roseanne all fit this profile. Assertors tend to be attracted to jokes and pointed humour. Look at the Judy Carter book I mentioned above, or try a stand-up comedy class.

Contemplators are task-oriented but more indirect and analytical. Humorists like Steven Wright, Woody Allen, and Ellen De Generes fit this profile. They like witty one-liners, observations, and irony. Like Narrators, they are low-key, but can just as easily win over an audience with their intellectual style of humour. Work through the exercises in *Comedy Writing Step by Step* by Gene Perret (Samuel French, 1990) for practice.

These styles, of course, are highly generalized but allow a good overview of how personality affects humour. Most people display qualities of more than one style. This is ideal for a speaker, since you not only want to remain true to yourself but also attract the variety of styles you will find in your audience. When you can easily switch between styles, or better yet, use them all at once, you know you have attained the Holy Grail of all humour styles, which I call the **Creator**.

Try the Humour Style Inventory Test. It is free. Just e-mail your request to: **info@yeseducationsystems.com** .

Carla Rieger
YES Education Systems
Ste. 138, 2906 West Broadway
Vancouver, BC V6K 2G8
P: 604-267-2381
F: 604-222-2267
info@yeseducationsystems.com
www.yeseducationsystems.com

About Carla Rieger

Carla Rieger is an expert in breaking down barriers to communication. Through humour, metaphor, and conflict resolution she helps leaders create and re-build important relationships. She is the owner of **YES Education Systems**, a Vancouver-based consulting firm. She is the author of two booklets: *Speaking on the Funny Side of the Brain* and *7½ Ways to Get Your Grouch*

Potato Off the Sofa. Her two manuals, *Captivate Your Audience* and *The Power of Laughter,* also help leaders add a powerful creative edge to their management toolkit.

For other articles on presenting skills or to find out about one-on-one coaching check out **www.yeseducationsystems.com** .

Fifty-one Platform Tips

by Geoffrey X. Lane

1. Always be yourself,whether you are a leader, a manager, a coach, a parent, an administrator, or a president. Your most important resource is the people you lead and manage, and the crucial element of your success (in reaching your goals) is your skill and ability to influence, inspire, motivate and encourage people.

The Magic of Enthusiasm

2. Enthusiasm is contagious and so is low energy! Let your audience know that you're committed to your ideas and that you're excited about them. They'll not only see your enthusiasm, they will feel it.

3. Enthusiasm is not the exclusive domain of a coach's pep talk or of a hard-sell delivery. You may speak softly, with heartfelt enthusiasm. You may be enthusiastically silent.

4. If it's important enough to talk about, there's some room for enthusiasm. So here's the idea: if you can't muster at least a small amount of real conviction for the subject of your talk, perhaps someone else should give it. After all, isn't a lack of enthusiasm or lack of interest a major reason why people change their jobs?

5. Act enthusiastic so your audience knows how you *feel* about your topic. The audience doesn't know your intentions. They can only judge you by your actions.

6. One of the most powerful results of giving a presentation with sincere enthusiasm is the look on the faces of your listeners. You'll notice appreciation, surprise and genuine delight. In today's world of advanced communication technology there is a renewed demand for old-fashioned person-to-person messages. After all, we're still human beings, animals that can speak to each other.

7. So you want to speak like a professional. Then get up there and say something that will make them lose track of time and forget everything else in their world except what you're telling them. Give them something to remember.

Platform Basics

8. The number one protection against anxiety is knowing your subject. Be over-prepared and you'll naturally feel better about your presentation.

9. Talk to one person at a time. Literally look directly into the eyes of one listener at a time, just as you would do in a normal day-to-day conversation. This might be difficult at first if you're used to scanning and avoiding eye contact, but it's worth the effort to acquire this basic habit of effective speech.

10. Stand up straight. Correct posture makes it easier for you to breathe, which in turn makes it easier for you to get your words out naturally—it gives you the appearance of having confidence.

11. Don't rely on drugs or alcohol to calm your nerves. Side effects like slowed reactions, slurred speech and hazy memory decrease your professionalism.

12. Know your opening line and your closing line. Know exactly where you want to go, having written your last sentence first. Practice your opening statement: it'll get you going. It's take-off time!

13. Practice affirming self-talk. Just before you get up to speak, hold your position and say to yourself, "I know what I'm going to say, and I'm glad for the chance to say it."

Keeping the Audience's Attention

14. Speak up. Talk a little louder than you think you have to. Most people speak far too softly so it sounds like they're mumbling. Speaking up also helps you calm anxiety or nervousness.

15. Use illustrations. Listeners' minds are hungry for pictures. Give them something to see. Use analogies and stories so they can visualize along with you. Use first-person stories whenever possible. The audience perks up when they hear phrases like, "The other day I..." or "I have found from my own experience..." or "A friend of mine once told me..."

16. Pause occasionally. Pauses are perhaps the most effective technique for regaining the attention of an audience. Most speakers don't use this powerful tool because the silence seems deafening—*to them.* However, the audience welcomes the pause. They usually relax and re-focus. Try it and you'll see all eyes looking back to you for your next statement.

17. Save handouts until after your presentation. If you give people materials at the beginning of your talk they'll read them instead of paying attention to you.

18. Use rhetorical questions like "What would you think if...?" You don't expect anyone to answer these questions out loud. But rhetorical questions have the effect of forcing people to respond mentally, hence keeping them on track with you.

Opening Remarks

19. Find an interesting opening statement or compelling first sentence. A bright Texan once said, "If you haven't struck oil in three minutes, stop boring." I would apply the same maxim to speeches—you have between thirty seconds and three minutes to convince the audience that you've got something interesting to say. One source you can use for ideas is *The Great Book of Inspiring Quotations: Motivational Sayings For All Occasions* by Peter Klavora and Dave Chambers (Sport Book Pub, 2001).

20. Avoid asking a question as an opener unless you've set it up as a rhetorical thought-provoking question for your audience, and you know in advance what the response will be. Otherwise you'll be risking offbeat, off-target, irrelevant and distracting comments or reactions.

21. Unless it is a formal occasion, you don't have to thank the person introducing you or thank the audience for coming. If you do, it often seems insincere. It will be a pleasant surprise for your listeners if you jump right in to your powerful opening sentence—and it will automatically identify you as a no-nonsense, passionate, compelling speaker.

22. Pause before you open your mouth to speak. Focus your eyes on one person in the audience, preferably someone about halfway to the back or in the first ten rows. The pause will get the audience's attention. Then direct your attention to someone in the middle of the room, as this will automatically cause you to speak louder than if you looked at somebody in the front row.

23. Stay on track. Don't risk losing the effect of your planned opening statement by trying to respond to the remarks of the previous speaker. It is a better plan to stick with your rehearsed opening, no matter how tempting it might be to change it.

24. Make your opening statement relate to business, not to the audience or the city where you're speaking. Such off-topic references may be appropriate in the middle of your talk. But if you've been asked to speak because you're an expert on a business topic, start on a businesslike note.

Closing Remarks

25. Don't sit down until you've told the audience what you want them to do. Presumably you weren't just talking to be nice, so tell them specifically what action they are expected to take. If, however, you *are* just talking to be nice, you are giving a social talk, even if it's to a business audience. In this situation simply end with a pleasant remark.

26. A welcome closing for the average business audience is one that comes a little ahead of schedule. Don't rush to finish early. Plan in advance to do so. Plan to end a few minutes early because if you go more than ten minutes past your time, you're in serious danger of losing your listeners. A tip you can use to stay on time is to break down your presentation into modules or digestible segments of ten to twelve minutes, each with its own key point.

27. If you plan to take questions after your presentation, the transition to questions will be your close. Therefore, plan a logical conclusion before you accept questions and save a minute or two at the end of the questions for a brief recap.

28. Bring back your best visual to accompany your closing remarks. This will give your audience both verbal and visual reinforcement of your central theme. Of course, knowing in advance that you're going to return to the key visual will also keep you focused on your conclusion throughout the presentation.

29. When you're preparing your talk, begin by outlining the conclusion, last sentence

first. This is the last thing they'll hear and the part they're most likely to remember. Many successful trial lawyers use this technique: they write their final argument first and then line up the evidence that best supports it and proves it to the jury.

Handling Questions and Answers

30. Sometimes the hardest part of a Q&A is getting people to participate. To encourage questions from your audience, break the ice by bringing up easy, conversational questions related to your subject. This is especially true with large audiences because no one wants to be first. Once the first person speaks, other questions will follow.

31. Ask people to wait to get their questions answered. Unless you designed your talk to be interrupted, let the audience know in advance that you're saving plenty of time for questions and answers at the end. Ask them to hold their questions until that time.

32. It's a good idea to repeat each question so the entire audience knows exactly what question you're answering. This is especially important with audiences of thirty or more people. Repeating it also gives you valuable thinking time.

33. Do not change the contextual or emotional meaning of a question. If you do, the audience will interpret this as unwillingness or inability to answer. Always repeat it out loud just as it was asked. Look directly at the person asking you the question and make sure he or she is finished before you start your answer.

During your answer, don't look at the questioner, but talk to the rest of the audience. If you direct your attention only to the questioner, you'll lose the audience's attention.

34. What if a previous questioner comes back for a more thorough answer? If it's your sale, client or boss, you already know what to do! If it's a nitpicker, be polite and give some additional information but don't get bogged down. If he or she persists, say that you'll be happy to meet with them afterwards for a longer discussion of that specific point.

35. Let the audience know when you're wrapping it up by announcing that you have time for *only one more question.* Be specific. If you intend to take two or more, tell them. But don't say "one or two more"—that sounds indecisive.

Using Visual Aids

36. Less is more. Use a few well-conceived, memorable visuals rather than many ordinary, boring charts or slides.

37. Keep the number of words per visual to a minimum. Use headlines only—better still, use short phrases or single words in bold type that can be clearly seen from the back row.

38. Use colour to highlight key points.

39. Explain exactly what each visual means so the audience doesn't have to guess. Even if it's fairly obvious what's on the chart, it's a good habit to reiterate it verbally, thus adding reinforcement to the key points.

40. When possible, use your hand to point to visuals. Many speakers misuse pointers, especially the retractable type. Have you ever noticed how distracting it is when a speaker plays with a pointer?

41. After you're through with a visual, move on. Don't give the audience anything to distract them from what you're saying now. This is particularly true if you're using overhead transparencies: turn the projector light out. If you're using an electronic slide presentation such as a liquid crystal display, just move it ahead.

Introducing Another Speaker

42. The key to an effective introduction is to give the audience a logical reason why the speaker was asked to be there. This usually has nothing to do with where he or she went to school or how many kids they've got. Tell the audience that they're about to hear from an expert and then relay the information that makes the speaker the expert, such as academic or business qualifications, or how much experience he or she has had. Find this out from the speaker before you start.

43. The major exception to the "logical reason" rule is for a testimonial or an award introduction. In this case, where the honoree or recipient is going to give an acceptance speech, the introduction is a mini-speech in itself. Your best plan is to get a detailed résumé from the individual. Then, if you don't know the person, interview him or her by telephone to get some additional interesting material. Even better, interview one or two acquaintances of the person and build a personal profile—because when you're giving an introduction of this kind it's usually a testimonial to the character and qualities of the human being you are introducing.

44. Don't say, "Our guest speaker needs no introduction." This is foolish if you're there to do an introduction. Be different. Come right out with the speaker's name: "Mary Smith is not only a key executive of ___, she is a leading authority on ___." Everybody knows (usually from a printed program) what her name is, so why pretend you're building to a surprise by waiting until the end of the introduction to give the speaker's name? Say it up front and go from there.

45. Double-check information you get from résumés and newspaper clippings. Facts change. People get divorced or widowed; change job titles, affiliations, political parties; gain new resources; create new headlines.

46. If you're introducing a colleague who's well known to most of the attendees, use the opportunity to say something new about him or her. Part of your job is to get the speaker off to a good start, and even old friends appreciate thoughtful introductions.

Incorporating Humour

47. The most natural expression of humour is the simple smile. Since most smiles are started by other smiles, make it a point to smile at least a couple of times during your talk—especially at the beginning. By relaxing, you'll naturally be more humorous.

48. Don't worry about deliberately incorporating humour. Most speakers can find something naturally funny to laugh at during a talk, like an upside-down slide or a Freudian slip, or even forgetting your own name! Or it might be something humorous that members of the audience throw in, intentionally or not, during a Q&A period. The point is, don't take yourself too seriously. Your natural sense of humour will come through when you're relaxed and giving your speech.

49. What about jokes? One of America's top comedy writers, Bob Orbon, said in a *Wall Street Journal* article that he could guarantee five show-stopping belly laughs from any business audience if he did the research and wrote the jokes into a speech. His fee for the job: several thousand dollars. What if the client doesn't have that kind of budget? In this case Orbon recommended buying one of his joke books and taking your chances. I make the point that being a stand-up comedian is an art mastered by only a few lifetime professionals—and if you're not one of them, why risk making a fool of yourself in the attempt? I remember watching Bob Hope on the *Johnny Carson Show* practicing a joke in front of Carson, and saying, "What did you think?" To which Carson replied, "Well, it's not quite right." Bob Hope then revealed that he'd been practicing for several years to try to get the timing right on that particular joke and never did. If it can happen to Bob Hope it can happen to you.

50. If you feel you must tell a joke, try it out on a couple of associates who not only know the audience you plan to use it on, but know you well enough to tell you if it's not appropriate for the occasion. My advice: don't do it at all.

51. In contrast to jokes, amusing incidents and stories from real life are sometimes quite appropriate. The key is timing. Tell the story at the right point in your talk, tie it into the business theme of your presentation and tell it *briefly*.

Geoffrey X. Lane
Lane Consulting Group Inc.
566-916 West Broadway
Vancouver, BC V5Z 1K7
P: 604-877-0089
F: 604-877-0029
geoffrey@geoffreyxlane.com
www.geoffreyxlane.com

About Geoffrey X. Lane

Since 1973 Geoffrey has been helping people overcome their fear of public speaking, to become effective communicators and to increase their sales results. An accredited Professional Speaker, he has developed the tools and philosophy that have enabled thousands of people to improve their lives.

Geoffrey began his sales and presentation career at Redken Laboratories, becoming a regular keynote speaker at trade shows throughout Canada, the USA and Australia.

Later, he joined Context Associated, a professional and personal development and leadership training organization. At Context he facilitated the Excellence Series and became respected and noted for the inspirational and humorous learning environments he created. As a result, people demanded his coaching and wanted insights into his techniques. Providing such services began to take up most of his time, and led to the development of Geoffrey's workshops, columns and a book.

Today his résumé includes a series of workshops with an impressive client list of CEOs, organizations and those inspired to speak publicly. His workshops focus on practical techniques that enable his clients to persuade and communicate with dramatically increased power and clarity.

In addition to his workshops and seminars, Geoffrey is a frequent lecturer for the UBC commerce executive education program and the UBC MBA program.

- Professional Speaker, author of *NuSpeak: Become a Powerful Speaker* (Berkana Books, 1999)

- Columnist, *Vancouver Sun* business section

- Presentation skills coach to the successful Vancouver 2010 Olympic bid

- Professional Member, Canadian Association of Professional Speakers

- Fast Track Director, BC Chapter, Canadian Association of Professional Speakers

For more information, see Geoffrey's web site at **www.geoffreyxlane.com** .

To subscribe to the GXL e-mail newsletter, go to: **www.geoffreyxlane.com/be_informed/ newsletter.htm** .

Keynote or Training: What's the Difference?

by Cheryl Cran

There I was, doing my first keynote in 1994, and all I saw looking back at me was a sea of completely expressionless faces. When it was over I kept reviewing the speech trying to figure out why I hadn't hit the mark. Based on my background in finance and training I had tried to load the presentation with facts, figures and messages of "you must do this or else", and what I received back from the audience was, "So what?" Now, years later, I realize that in my nervousness I had forgotten the passion, and focused instead on looking and sounding intelligent as well as trying to jam it all into a one-hour format.

Many speakers want to become full time keynoters due to perceived glamour or prestige. There are other speakers today who combine keynotes and training seminars as well as coaching and consulting in a well-rounded speaking practice. My personal style incorporates a diversified approach to the speaking business that includes all forms of presentations. What I am focusing on is being a better presenter for both keynotes and training seminars and therefore getting more business, referrals and bureau bookings.

You might have asked yourself what the difference is between training and keynoting, or perhaps you believe that there isn't a fundamental difference between the two. Professional speakers have varied opinions about the right way to conduct an all-day training session or the right way to keynote. The bottom line, from my perspective, is that there are many paths to a successful keynote or training day and there is no one way to succeed at either. Having said this, I am presenting the differences as I see them based on my experience as a professional speaker for the last ten years.

What a Keynote and an All-Day Seminar Have in Common

Although different, they have some similar characteristics that will more or less guarantee success at either keynoting or training. The similarities are:

- A strong open and a strong close are required
- The WIFT principle applies to both (**W**hat's **I**n It **F**or **T**hem)
- Both focus on the audience, their perspectives and their needs
- Each provides specific calls to action: the speaker tells them what they need to do as a result of hearing the speech.

Now let's look at the fundamental differences between keynotes and half-day or full-day seminars.

Keynotes

The timeframe for keynotes is typically one hour, although some keynotes can go to ninety minutes or two hours. Keynotes are exactly that: a "key note" meant to focus the audience on a particular theme, concept or call to action. Keynotes are often positioned at the opening of a conference, during a luncheon or at the close of a conference. Meeting planners want the speaker to encapsulate the theme of their conference into the presentation, and use knowledge and awareness of the issues facing those attending the conference.

Some keynoters will conduct a pre-program survey with a number of participants and attend conference functions to gather a good sense of who will be attending, what their issues are and what dynamics are going on within the attendees' industry. Others, like Janet Lapp, CSP, CPAE, do not do pre-program questionnaires. Janet's expertise is "change" and she prefers to gather her perceptions of the attendees by attending the prior evening's cocktail party, conference breakfast or luncheon.

For a keynote your message needs to be tight and concise. Ian Percy, CSP, CPAE, HoF says that for his keynotes he looks at his presentation through the audience's eyes and will ask himself questions like, "How will what I have to say here make an impact on those in the audience with what they are going through?" Ian also incorporates the logo of the conference into his Powerpoint presentation so that his presentation is visibly about them.

Alan Simmons, CSP, CPAE, HoF always asks himself the following while preparing for a keynote: "What will they know when it's over? What will they do when it's over?" Because keynote speakers only have an hour or two to connect with the audience you must be clear on the end result and build your keynote around your answers to Alan's two questions.

Keynotes require mega-doses of energy and passion. You need to "own the platform", stand large, and use large, expressive hand gestures and movements. The goal is to inspire and motivate those in the audience to move forward with energy and ideas for action. In an opening keynote your role is to set the tone for the entire conference. Meeting planners want a speaker to fire up the attendees so that they will completely engage in the conference: be full of energy, positive attitude and excitement about what the rest of the conference will provide.

In a closing keynote your role is to encapsulate the entire conference from opening to middle to end, and bring it all together with a closing message of what was learned and what attendees can do with what they learned. The goal is for the audience to leave inspired while reinforcing the value they received by attending the conference. A phenomenal closing keynoter can turn an average conference into a razzle-dazzle event by focusing on positive events throughout the conference.

A luncheon keynote often requires a humorous speaker. Meeting planners want to rev up their attendees to continue engaging in conference activities and to re-energize them for the remainder of the conference.

Because of the timeframe of a keynote I have learned to focus on three main "take aways" or "gems" for the audience. These are concepts or calls to action that are the core of a keynote. When I first did a keynote I found myself wanting to jam in all sorts of data, thinking that it was what the audience wanted or needed. Over time and with experience I have moved towards the "keep it simple" approach by sticking to three main ideas and then building the remainder of the keynote around those ideas.

Unless you are a humorist, opening with a joke is not always a good idea. David Sweet, the founding president of CAPS, has said that a strong keynote always opens with a powerful story and that personal stories are best. It is even more powerful if you tie your opening story into your closing, which is sometimes called the "wrap-around technique". By doing this you bring the audience back to you at the end, tying the entire speech together.

You may be asking about the structure of a keynote or struggling with where to start. There are a variety of ways to put your keynote together and I certainly do not profess to be the sole authority, or to imply that my method works for everyone. I will share with you the process I have learned from the masters in the business and then encourage you to make it your own for your success.

Keynote Structure Ideas

What I do is write my keynote out by hand to get my ideas, stories and concepts out of my mind and onto paper. Once I do that I look at what I've written to find my three main points within the keynote. I put those three points onto index cards and then write down key words that lead to stories I will use around each of the key points. I have over twenty possible personal stories I could use and, depending on the topic, audience or point I am making, I will choose the story that will fit best.

I choose which story I will open or close with and ensure that it fits within the context of the keynote or the theme of the conference. Once the key points and stories are in place I look for places where I can insert humour or a quick interactive exercise to keep the audience's energy level up. As to flow, I do not have this down to an exact science but I like to use a method similar to Doug Stephenson's. A one-hour keynote may look something like this:

- Opening story: seven minutes
- Interactive mini-exercise: three minutes
- Audience participation: two minutes
- Story: two minutes
- Call to action or point #1: two minutes
- Joke or humour: two minutes

Then repeat this cycle twice more, once for each of the other two key points. The total time for the above is about twenty minutes. Multiply that by three and you have one hour of keynote speaking time. This isn't what I would necessarily do every time but it has helped me to frame my keynotes and ensure I focus on the three main points of the message.

To Powerpoint or Not to Powerpoint

People have differing opinions on whether or not to use Powerpoint for keynotes. I have seen exceptional keynotes without it and also with it. Peter Legge, CSP, CPAE, HoF does not use Powerpoint and doesn't plan to. Peter is a storyteller and his stories are his message. He does a brilliant job of using the power of engaging storytelling to bring his audience with him, taking them through an emotional range from laughing to crying, so that by the end they are completely enthralled and moved by his presentation. Joe Malarkey, *aka* George Campbell, is another example. As a humorist he relies solely on his physical humour to make his point and it works tremendously well.

Someone who uses Powerpoint effectively in keynotes is Linda Tarrant, CSP, CPAE. I like how she incorporates sound into her presentation so it supports the points she is making. Linda Edgecombe also uses Powerpoint very effectively, showing pictures that everyone can relate to that support her stories or jokes. I think you need to ask yourself what you are most comfortable with and what would make the message more effective for your audience.

I have done keynotes with and without Powerpoint and I decide whether or not to use it based on what I am going to do in a particular situation. Sometimes I have nothing on which to base my decision other than my intuition about what would be most effective for that particular group.

Other Things to Keep in Mind

Handouts are optional when it comes to keynotes, as are props. Some keynoters like to provide Powerpoint handouts to their audiences, but I will say this: if you do, do not hand them out until the end of the keynote. Otherwise people will look at the handout rather than focus on the keynoter. Other keynoters leave a laminated bookmark with their main points on it, or some other item that can be taken away and remembered by the audience. This is an excellent marketing tool as well!

Props can be very powerful in a keynote and can come in many forms. I saw an outstanding luncheon keynote at last year's NSA convention in Orlando by Tim Gard, CSP. His keynote was on the humour of travel and he used chairs, suitcases, podiums and other props to make his points brilliantly. Your own body can be a prop, as Joe Malarkey shows his audiences. At his luncheon keynote at the 2002 CAPS conference in Vancouver, his thumbs-up with a super-sized grin said it all. There is no right or wrong: again, it is personal preference, although in my experience I have found that with most keynotes people don't expect a handout or props.

Training

The fundamental difference between keynotes and training is time. With a keynote you have a short period of time to make an impact, win over the audience and create passion and excitement, whereas a training day typically gives you four to six hours to establish a relationship with your audience. Training gives you the luxury of time to build a relationship with your audience, gain trust, and re-establish credibility if you have lost it during the presentation.

Training audiences expect that while being entertained they will receive content and practical ideas that they can implement. Speakers who do very well in the training aspect of the speaking business often refer to themselves as "edu-tainers". Today's audiences are highly educated and intelligent and already know a lot of what they are being trained to do. Therefore they want a trainer to be authentic and practical, giving them useful solutions and keeping them interested throughout the day.

I treat my training days as six one-hour keynotes. That means that within each hour of training I ensure there are practical and useful tools for the audience to take away, and mix that up with stories, humour and interaction. In a training day I like to include lots of activity and interaction to keep the audience engaged and learning all day. I like to vary my energy level in a training day and have found that I need to maintain high levels of energy to keep the audience with me.

I have personally spent the majority of my speaking career so far in one-day seminars and have found that there are certain things that will always work in creating a successful day.

Training Day Structure Ideas

As I mentioned, I treat my one-day seminars as six one-hour keynotes, with some variations. My first step is to build the training day and to prepare the handouts based on the teaching points for the session. Then I print off the handout and use the master copy as a "teaching copy" on which I put my notes/stories/jokes/ activities to refer to throughout the training day.

The outline for a one-day training for me might look something like this.

9:00:   Opening story that solidifies the WIFT for the audience

9:15:   What they can expect from the day, agenda review, content and value

9:20:   Icebreaker/group activity

9:25:   Debrief activity

9:30:   Story

9:35:   Content

9:50:   Joke or humorous activity

10:00: Content

10:15: Break

Then I repeat the cycle throughout the day. One thing that always works for me is that whenever I bring the group back from a break we do a mini-review of concepts we covered before the break and then use that to lead into new content as we move forward. After lunch is often a challenging time for participants because they have full bellies, are physically tired from sitting, and are getting brain tired. That is when I will have them do a group activity, or I will tell a story— or at around 2:00 or 2:30 I will get them up and moving around.

The important thing to remember about stories is that they have to make a point. If you tell stories for the sake of telling them you can lose the audience, since they are already asking themselves, "What's the point?" I was guilty of this! I would launch into a story I thought was wonderful and then would find in my evaluations that people felt my stories did not always make a point! I learned from the feedback and since then have made a concerted effort to ensure I have a point when telling a story.

When closing a training day I ramp up the energy again to review the entire agenda quickly and then tell a story related to the day's training, or I will use a quote that encapsulates what the day was about.

Facilitation of meetings is very different in that you are there to support a specific process or to obtain results customized for that group. I facilitate management retreats where the goal is to create new focus and encourage action to achieve benchmarks or targets. When facilitating you literally go where the group takes you. You act as a mediator between ideas and concepts that the group brings forward.

Facilitating may get uncomfortable. You not only have to be willing to address the issues that arise but you must also have the skill to keep the process on track and focused towards the mandate of the meeting. I truly enjoy facilitation because of the conflict involved, especially how creative ideas and breakthroughs for the group spring from it.

Visual Aids, Props and More

The other opportunity you have when training is that you can use a variety of ways to communicate your messages or to make your points. Trainers still use overheads because they are so flexible to use and the timing is more precise: you have a greater degree of control over when each slide goes on, or whether you use one at all. The only comment I will make in regard to using overheads is that you must ensure they look as professional as possible. Today's audiences are so used to Powerpoint that if they see shoddy overheads they will make negative assumptions about the presenter, which hinders credibility. When using overheads I make my slides from Powerpoint in full colour with pictures. I prefer to use Powerpoint for training because I can incorporate sound and video to emphasize a training point. I also still use flipcharts for groups of twenty or fewer as well as for facilitations.

In my opinion props are a requirement for a successful training day. I have used fruit, "silly slammers", Groucho Marx glasses, bouncy balls, Slinkies and other goofy things to help make a point and to bring more humour to the training day. In training you are an edu-tainer, so props help you give visual reinforcement of the teaching point you are making. Margaret Hope does a stellar job of using props in her presentations. I still have not forgotten one of her presentations, because of the way she was dressed (in a lab coat) and the final result of the "experiment" she did for the audience with a specific concoction that visually illustrated the concepts she had delivered. (The concoction is a secret that Margaret will only reveal in her presentations.)

So Now What?

Well, if you thought speaking was speaking, you were right. But there are things you need to keep in mind when preparing either a keynote or a training day. The main idea that has helped me is to make it all about them—the audience. When I first started out in my speaking career I have to admit it was more about me than about anyone else. I wanted to be seen as intelligent, witty and a great presenter. The truth is that as long as I focused on myself I was disconnecting from my audience. Once I made it about them— their needs, their issues and their concerns—I found myself relaxing more and becoming more authentic on the podium.

I hope I have given you some valuable tips that will help you with your keynoting and training career. The work you do is so important— the world needs you. Now get out there and speak!

Cheryl Cran
Synthesis At Work
Ste. 1000, 355 Burrard St.
Vancouver, BC V6C 2G8
P: 604-552-9640
Toll free: 877-900-5010
F: 604-552-8588
info@cherylcran.com
www.cherylcran.com

About Cheryl Cran

Cheryl Cran is the author of *Say What You Mean, Mean What You Say* and is a contributing author to the *Don't Sweat Stories*. She is an internationally renowned motivational speaker and communication expert, and works with corporations and associations to improve leadership, build teamwork, enhance customer care and manage change.

Cheryl motivates and inspires individuals and groups to reach higher, think more creatively and shift behaviours to create new and exciting results, both professionally and personally.

People who participate in Cheryl's sessions leave with shifted perspectives, renewed energy and actionable ideas. The result is increased personal power, enhanced communication abilities and better relationships. As individuals increase their personal power the corporations or associations they work for receive improved productivity, increased profits and more loyal customers.

Cheryl is the president of **Synthesis at Work**, a consulting firm dedicated to helping companies collaborate, communicate and accelerate. A successful entrepreneur since 1994, Cheryl has worked with a diverse range of industries such as finance groups, health care organizations, homebuilder companies, government, and associations. She has worked with both union and non-union sectors in business and government.

As an expert in interpersonal communication Cheryl has been interviewed on *The Vicki Gabereau Show* and *Urban Rush*. Her articles have been featured in *Business Woman Canada* magazine, *Selling Power* magazine and *BC Business* magazine. She was nominated as a YWCA Woman of Distinction in 2001 and named one of Vancouver's top speakers by the *Business in Vancouver* newspaper.

Cheryl is the 2003 president of the BC chapter of the Canadian Association of Professional Speakers and is a Certified Speaking Professional candidate.

The Courage to Keynote!

by David Gouthro

What is courage? And what does it have to do with keynoting? I'll define courage as an inner quality that becomes evident when one takes action where there is:

1. an uncertain or unpredictable outcome;
2. an emotion or feeling attached to the thought of the action; and
3. a positive value or belief which compels us to act—or in this case, speak.

Whenever we're about to step in front of a group we have a sense of what we hope to achieve—but there's no guarantee we'll do so. We have an emotional response to the thought of speaking. If the chances of failure seem slim, we might experience mild anxiety. If failure could result in major embarrassment, loss of face or perhaps even (gasp) revenue, our feeling might be closer to terror. What drives us to act in spite of the uncertainty and accompanying discomfort?

Simply put, values. When we have a strong belief about the "right" thing to say or do, we're compelled to speak. Experience tells me that professional speakers have an extremely strong sense of values—we know what is right for us! And it's usually to communicate something we're passionate about, believe in and wish to share.

What requires courage for one person may require little or none for another. Going rock climbing may take plenty of courage the first time. Questions like, "Is the equipment reliable? Are my belayers competent? What happens if I slip?" may shadow our adventure. Do we value growth or adventure sufficiently to move us beyond the initial uncertainty and accompanying fear? If so, predictability increases as we gain experience, and our anxiety decreases with each attempt. The courage required to climb the tenth time is less than the first—and by the hundredth climb the notion of courage may not even be relevant. I believe the same process applies to speakers. At least it did to me!

I made the shift from training to keynote speaking with relative ease. Looking back, it was because I really wasn't doing anything courageous. I wasn't taking any significant risks. I simply adjusted my training style to shorter time periods. Instead of running a one- to three-day workshop, I was jamming a subset of the same material into an hour. Same stories, cartoons and overhead transparencies. Nothing to it. Unfortunately that statement was very true—NOTHING to it.

Fortunately I received some advice on how to become a real keynoter, to speak without slides. Gasp! Although I was allegedly a motivational speaker, I wasn't in a hurry to take that one on! I slowly (and painfully) reduced the number of transparencies I relied on. I began to tell a few stories from memory. No big deal for many of you, but I was a nervous wreck. I was petrified I would leave something out and do a disservice to the original author (with attribution, of course), the story, and the audience. I didn't feel my own experience would be as interesting as someone else's.

Then one dark day in May I took the plunge! No transparencies, flipcharts, or stories to read, and an almost off-the-scale anxiety level about ending early and having too little to say. Courage was the last thing on my mind. Survival was pretty high up the list, though!

Well, I survived the experience. Definitely not my best work, but I did it! My sense of accomplishment was tremendous. Just this once I indulged myself and focused primarily on me rather than my client. I'd relied entirely on my head, heart and soul—and it felt GREAT! My only regret is that it didn't happen twenty years ago.

Looking back, my experience met all the criteria for courage even though being courageous was the furthest thing from my mind. There was an uncertain outcome. I wasn't terrorized, but I was certainly anxious. The value that drove me that particular day? Growth. In this case I was willing to risk failure to provide better service and value to future clients.

Do I still get anxious? Absolutely, but less so. Now I'm much more motivated to step into the unknown in my speaking practice.

The following could very well require courage for a professional speaker:

- Speaking in front of huge groups;
- Publicly expressing an unpopular opinion;
- Speaking "naked" (no A/V or other props);
- Taking on an exceptionally challenging assignment;
- Turning down a much-needed speaking opportunity because it doesn't feel right;
- Deciding to make professional speaking your sole source of income;
- Delivering a totally new topic for the first time; or
- Speaking right after a popular speaker.

Simply reading about courage doesn't build it, though. Choose one of these actions (or create one of your own) today and take that first step by *acting* on it. Take one small step—you will survive! And you'll find your willingness to take ever-increasing risks will grow, as will your confidence and competence.

Speaking with courage is a wonderful source of fulfillment and satisfaction. Succeed or fail, we can't help but gain as individuals while providing inspiration for others to act with courage, too. The opportunity and choice are ours!

David Gouthro
The Consulting Edge: Movers &
  Shakers, Inc.
23-1551 Johnston St.
Vancouver, BC V6H 3R9
P: 604-685-6858
Toll free: 800-685-6818
F: 604-685-6242
dgouthro@theconsultingedge.com
www.theconsultingedge.com

About David Gouthro

As president of **The Consulting Edge**, David Gouthro possesses a rare talent for infusing courage and innovation into audiences engaged in his programs and presentations. For over twenty years he has been encouraging others to "seize the day" and develop greater personal effectiveness, regardless of their personal or organizational circumstances.

David has a knack for inspiring people to take up the constant pursuit of knowledge and the skills they need to achieve success. His energetic and playful approach incorporates variety, humour and fun, and has earned him a reputation as facilitator and speaker of choice for a wide variety of private, public and not-for-profit organizations throughout North America.

Particularly commended for his unwavering client focus, David is highly motivated to help others succeed—both personally and professionally. In addition to being sharp, stimulating, and engaging, he remains sensitive to the unique needs and circumstances of each distinct group with which he has the privilege of working. His thought-provoking sessions stimulate participation and actions that lead individuals and organizations to greater satisfaction and growth.

An avid learner himself, David deeply values improving his own knowledge and performance by keeping abreast of the latest advancements in leadership and organizational development. Clients benefit from his continuous learning with expert access to the most current and effective organizational change technologies. As a keynote speaker, David delivers practical concepts that address real-life issues that impede growth and prosperity. He does this through entertaining, educational sessions brimming with energy and fun.

David takes time to really understand the business of each of his clients. This fulfils the client's requirement to be understood and David's desire to learn and provide as much value as possible.

David is a member of the Vancouver Board of Trade, BC Chamber of Commerce, Canadian Association of Professional Speakers, International Society for Performance Improvement, International Association of Facilitators, and the BC Association of Facilitators. He is also a founding member of the soon-to-be-famous Vancouver Noseflute Ensemble!

To Bureau or Not to Bureau

by Linda Edgecombe

It seems most speakers I meet would do almost anything to be listed with and work alongside a speakers' bureau. I have to say that I enjoy some really satisfying relationships with "my" eight or so bureaus, and presently about 50 to 60 percent of my bookings come from speakers' bureaus. Over the years, as my business has grown, so have the number of bookings and the number of bureaus I partner with. But it must be said that not all speakers and trainers are a good fit with bureaus.

First and foremost I think that many speakers, me included, came to the bureau side of the speaking business with the wrong motivation in mind. I hear so many of my colleagues say, "I am really not any good at marketing and I would love someone to market and book me instead." My comment on this way of thinking is that bureaus are not there to market you. They are there to find the best fit for their clients.

Every bureau operates with a slightly different philosophy. Some regard their clients (corporations, associations and professional meeting planners) as their most important relationship while others feel that both speakers and the groups who book speakers are equal partners in building and maintaining their business. Some bureaus have in fact supported a speaker in the event of a complaint. The key is to interview each potential bureau about its approach to building strong business relationships.

Speakers are plentiful, so finding a speaker to fill the spot is usually never a problem. What you must become, before you ever get in the door of a bureau, is an expert at marketing yourself. Speakers simply must have their own business strategies in place before initiating a partnership with a bureau. You need to know what it's like to work with a client over time and negotiate deals. Then you can build relationships with bureaus.

Some Basic Terminology

The first thing every speaker needs to understand is that there is a difference between a speakers' bureau, an agent and a management company. While all three take a percentage of the business that they bring to you, each serves a slightly different purpose. Unless you are a famous person (and if you are, you will already know this), it's not likely that you'll have an agent to book you into speaking events. Agents work mainly with celebrities, and negotiate all bookings for that person, whether for speaking engagements or other activities.

Like an agent, a management company will handle all business that comes to you, whether that business comes from a bureau or from clients who call you directly. But a management company will also be involved in the administration of your office, handling such tasks as invoicing and filing.

A speakers' bureau works with clients (companies, associations and not-for-profits) that hold events throughout the year. The aim of the bureau is to help these clients find speakers for their meetings. That's where you come in. In general, bureaus are speakers' clients—very important clients but clients nonetheless. Some bureaus may provide services similar to those of an agent or a management company, handling all business that is directed to you. This is what you would call an "exclusive" relationship with a bureau.

You might find a recent survey conducted by the NSA interesting (published June 2003):

- 55.5% of members don't work with speakers' bureaus at all

- 25% of the members said they get 1 to 10 percent of their bookings from bureaus

- 5.3% of members get 11 to 20 percent of their bookings from bureaus

As a quick summary, 86% of NSA and CAPS members get 20 percent or less of their bookings from speakers' bureaus.

For me this says all speakers must have their own sales and marketing strategies instead of depending on bureaus.

Steps to Get You in the Bureau's Door

Where do you find lists of speakers' bureaus and agents?

If you want to start by connecting to bureaus in your area, you can go to a web site that features various Canadian and American bureaus, such as the one for IASB (International Association of Speakers' Bureaus) at **www.iasbweb.org** . You can also go to this site: **www.expertspace.com/resource_guide/ speakers_bureaus.html** .

You can find literally hundreds of bureaus listed on the Web if you search with the phrase "speakers' bureaus". Another way to get a comprehensive list of bureaus is to purchase it from Lilly Walters. You can get all the info you can imagine on speakers' bureaus in North America at:

http://www.motivational-keynote-speakers.com/speakersbureauscontact.html .

Other Resources from Lilly Walters

Lilly has also compiled valuable information about speakers and bureau relationships in a report titled "How to Be a Bureau's Favorite Speaker". The report currently costs $12.99 (US). Content includes:

- What bureaus want
- Why bureaus' favourites are their favourites
- What annoys bureaus about speakers
- Unusual ways to get noticed by bureaus
- Sticky ethical issues with bureaus

You can also purchase an entire bureau package that includes all of the above and over 300 links to bureaus for $59.00 (US).

Once you have lists of bureaus, you can research the types of speakers each of the bureaus is currently booking.

When I introduce myself to any new bureau, I make a phone call to speak with a real voice. I ask if I may send them my current promo package, and a video. I now have everything as an electronic file, so I ask if it is appropriate for me to send files of all my promo material too, on disk or by e-mail.

I know that working with bureaus is a "plant the seed" process, where you nurture the relationship and eventually start to reap the benefits from the initial contact. It is also critical for most bureau reps to see you in action personally. So make sure you invite bureaus out to see you when you are in their area. Most bureaus tell me that they really need to see a speaker to "get" a speaker. I know your package tells them everything about you and your video gives them a great impression of how you are on your feet, but understanding and feeling how an audience responds to a speaker is critical before any bureau rep can really market you to clients. It is personal and it is about connecting. This client, right speaker: that's the recipe they are looking for.

Finding a Match

What's perfect for one speaker may not be perfect for another. So how do you find the perfect bureau for *you*? You may want to ask some of your colleagues what bureaus they are currently working with and what their relationships are like with those bureaus. Make sure you ask speakers whose opinions you respect and whose approach to their speaking practice is similar to yours.

You can also contact bureaus directly. A great place to start is with some non-aggressive qualifying questions. Here is a short list you can use to see if you are a good fit for any given bureau you are pursuing, and vice versa.

1. Is this a good time for you?

2. Do you book (motivational, business, technology) speakers? Are you accepting speakers right now? (If yes, go to question three. If no, go on to the next bureau.)

3. What do you look for in a speaker?

4. What is the fee range at which you book your speakers? (Based on the answer you receive, you may wish to provide the bureau with your fee range to indicate your suitability.)

5. I have bureau-friendly promotional material, including videos, "one-sheets", and copies of books I have written. May I send them to you for review?

6. When would you like me to follow up with you?

7. I am in (your town) in (month). Can we meet for coffee? Or, I would like to invite you out to see me speak on (date). Any leads I generate from that engagement I would be more than happy to pass along to you for follow-up.

What Bureau-Friendly Really Means

Here's how I have made my materials (promotional materials and handouts) bureau-friendly. I have two promotional packages that I use. One has all my personal contact information on my speaker's package, video, CD-ROM, electronic files, etc. The other has a specific bureau's current contact information on it. I customize packages for each of the bureaus I work closely with. I have their web site addresses, e-mail addresses and phone numbers printed on the packages, CD-ROMs, videos and other items. I also have some materials with no contact information on them, in case a group or bureau wants to add its own.

When a bureau books me for an event, I change my handouts to reflect the contact info for the bureau booking me for that event. I even have business cards with my name printed on them for a few of the bureaus for which I do a fair bit of work, and hand those out at events.

Pulling Together Your Bureau Promotional Pieces

Although I have been booked by a few bureaus that never actually saw me speak or even saw my promotional video, that is highly unusual. So I'd like to suggest a list of requirements to consider as you get your marketing pieces together.

1. A sharp "One-Page"

This is literally a promotional piece about you: a bio (including a photo), your topics, your products, your current clients and some of their feedback, all on one double-sided sheet of paper. Most bureaus will tell you that they fax or e-mail their clients these sheets and it's from these that clients ask for full promo packages. As I mentioned, these sheets can either be faxed or e-mailed. So make this piece in both black and white and colour.

2. Speaker's packages

There are as many variations on this promotional piece as there are speakers. What I have done over the years is to look at who my competition is for an event: that is, whose names are being considered along with mine. I want to look like I am a viable option.

Start by asking who spoke last year and who they are considering for this year. See if you are typically going up against the same group of speakers. Then plan your marketing materials to look like you belong in the company you are keeping.

If you are just starting out, you don't need to spend thousands of dollars on packages. Avoid preprinting insert pages: print as you go. Find a package that you can grow into for a couple of years.

Do not print your contact information on your insert pages. This is where the "bureau-friendly" info goes. Customize your insert pages to the bureau you are working with.

Note to female speakers: I have surveyed my bureaus to find out if my male colleagues get booked more, less or at the same frequency as women. Their response has been that men in fact do get booked more frequently. With that in mind, I designed my package with professionalism at the forefront. I spent some money on all my promotional pieces to say that I am very serious about being a part of this industry. Mind you, as a speaker I'm not a very serious person at all!

3. Good promotional video

Some of the bureaus I work with say that this piece still stands out as the first and most important promotional item. It must capture you at your best, and show that you can hold your own with large and small audiences. One bureau went so far as to say that the funnier you come across in your video, the more bookings you get. So show all your funniest clips!

When speaking to prospective bureaus, you might want to ask what length of video they want, but you are not going to customize your videos for every bureau. It's just too costly. A good rule of thumb would be to show your best stuff up front for about ten minutes and then show a longer clip at the end in case a client wants to see you in full swing. You will be short-listed from the first ten minutes and booked based on your last twenty to thirty minutes.

4. Promotional CD-ROM

There is definitely a trend towards putting all your promotional materials on CD-ROM, but the Canadian bureaus I spoke with indicated that they still prefer, as do most of their clients, to view a speaker on video. So if you are trying to decide whether to spend your marketing dollars on CD-ROM production or on self-publishing a book, get the book printed.

5. Web sites

Bureaus have told me that although each speaker needs a web site, they tend not to send their clients there but may use it as additional promotional material to nail down a contract. In summary, you do need a web site. It is industry standard to have one, but not all bureaus use them to promote you. They send their clients to their own web sites, where you are listed.

Exclusive, or the Partner of Many?

Although I have been asked to take exclusive contracts with a few of my bureaus, I have chosen not to. I currently work with several great bureaus and enjoy nurturing those partnerships. In contrast, I have colleagues who have chosen to be exclusive with a bureau because it frees them up from having to negotiate contracts and book their own travel, and they have said it reduces their stress levels. Their exclusive relationships are like an extension of their office support.

My bureaus have indicated that there is a trend away from exclusive speakers and that speakers themselves have initiated the trend. Individual sales reps at each bureau are the ambassadors who book you, and getting on to a short list is often based on the relationship you have nurtured with that sales agent.

There's no right or wrong here. Just stick with whatever works for you and your business needs.

Top of Mind Strategies

Belinda Miller-Foey of CAN**SPEAK** Presentations in Vancouver contributes these top ten things a speaker can do to be on a bureau's "A" list.

How to Break Through

1. Treat the bureau as a partner, not a competitor.

Remember, even if the bureau's sales agent hasn't booked you yet, you can assume the bureau is working hard on your behalf if it has accepted you on its roster. Be sure to contact the bureau regularly and ask your bureau partner how you can help get yourself booked.

Turn leads over to your bureau partner if you're not available for a potential engagement. Most bureaus will provide you with a finder's fee on new business resulting from your lead. And you can be sure that when you're thinking of your bureau partner, then you have the bureau thinking about you!

2. Turn over a client to a bureau you want to work with.

Speaker Joe Calloway's advice on the single best way to get bureaus to book you is as follows.

"Take a job that comes directly to you. Do the job through a bureau that you've been wanting to work with. Just give it to them with a full commission. Then have the client call the bureau with spin-off bookings. You are now in business with that bureau!"

3. Keep in frequent contact ("out of sight, out of mind").

Keep bureaus informed of your new topics, articles, book releases, etc. Stay in touch by sending a new client testimonial or information about successes that you've had in a particular industry. Chances are that the bureau has many contacts within the same industry and can apply the same strategy with similar success.

Fostering the Relationship

4. Go the extra mile with the bureau's client.

Call the client immediately upon receiving the bureau contract to set up a briefing interview at a time convenient to the client. This allows both parties to put faces to names and start building rapport. The briefing interview also lets you customize your presentation to fit the client's needs and meet all deadlines. You must know more about the client's business than any other speaker they've had before. This is your biggest competitive advantage!

Keep expenses as low as possible within the contract requirements. And here's a new trend: be willing to provide the bureau with an all-inclusive fee. Clients today are looking for the bottom line, and this approach speaks to their need.

Most important, deliver a memorable program. The bureau will know that you've gone the extra mile when the client says you were easy to work with, did a fabulous job and wants to book you again!

5. Be a bureau's ambassador.

This means that you've got to wear the bureau hat. Acknowledge your bureau partner during client pre-event conference calls and when meeting the client on-site. Any handouts must be "bureau-friendly" (with bureau contact numbers and web site address).

6. Always bring business back to the bureau that booked you.

All repeat business and spin-off business that results from a bureau-booked engagement must be referred back to the bureau. Have a strategy for getting those spin-off leads—if you give a speech and you don't get any referrals from it, then go back to work on the speech! Applause and standing ovations are great but repeat and referral business is what counts.

Keep in mind that bureaus will exhaust all efforts to book the speaker that gave them the lead before they recommend another speaker.

Keeping the Momentum

7. Show appreciation for the business bureaus bring you and keep bureau business confidential.

Call the bureau sales agent after each event to personally thank him or her for the business and provide your feedback on the event. Keep bookings confidential. Do not share specific client information about business resulting from one bureau with another.

8. Be easy to reach.

Have a live person available at all times to give the bureau your availability or to set up a client conference call. Respond to bureau requests for customized proposals or reference letters with same-day turnaround.

9. Provide material that is current and bureau-friendly.

Regularly monitor your profile on bureau sites and update your topics and key benefits regularly. Clients want to hire "experts", so clearly define your expertise and the benefits to hiring you.

Improve your delivery style on a continuous basis. Have a video that accurately conveys what you do in live presentations; again, make it "bureau-friendly".

8. Offer quality product.

Be willing to provide product (books, CDs, audio tapes, posters) at the sales agent's discretion to seal the deal when negotiating with their clients for a major multi-city tour or multiple booking deal.

Conclusion

What I have found over the years is that as I have grown, so have my relationships with my bureaus. Every bureau that I partner with knows me, knows about my family and the kind of life I strive for. Together we make the business relationship as beneficial to each other as possible. I really don't think there are any real right or wrong answers here. Just growth. Here's to you growing your business.

Linda Edgecombe
Learning Edge Resources
Corporation
2102 Bowron St.
Kelowna, BC V1V 2L6
P: 250-868-9601
F: 250-868-9740
www.lindaedgecombe.com
info@lindaedgecombe.com

About Linda Edgecombe

Linda Edgecombe is an internationally renowned speaker, trainer and consultant. She is a best-selling author who energizes every room as she leads people to loosen up, lighten the load and laugh. Her audiences are motivated and shown how they can shift their perspectives on life, work and themselves. Change has never been this painless!

As a professional with a degree in physical education, Linda brings twenty years of recreation, employee wellness, lifestyle and corporate consulting experience to her programs and her clients. She was a consultant for PARTICIPACTION, promoting healthy living to Canadians, and is known for being one of the country's most popular speakers.

Inside the laughter, Linda's audiences are inspired to find the meaning in what they do and let go of what's not working. Her message is as

welcome as a deep belly laugh and as profound as a good look in the mirror.

"I've got this great idea for a book!": Getting Published

by Frances McGuckin

"If you're a speaker, you *must* publish a book!" Perhaps you've heard this comment before. Many speakers hang their hopes on publishing to gain further credibility in their field and to generate extra income. Starry-eyed and brimming with excitement, their response is often, "Yes, I've got this great idea for a book!" There's no doubt that being a published author adds tremendous credibility to your reputation as a speaker and as "the expert". Although many people dream of publishing, few realize the continuous hard work, aggressive marketing—and money—involved.

Completing a non-fiction work takes copious time. Not everyone was born to write, so honing your writing skills is a mandatory requirement. If you can't put your message into a readable format, readers won't finish the book. The editing process—even before a professional editor looks at your book—can involve rewriting the manuscript many times.

Each sentence must be structured without a clutter of unnecessary words. Each paragraph must lead into another. Each page must be visually interesting and well laid out. Each chapter must flow into the next. Your messages should be clear. That's just the start.

This chapter will walk you through the basics of understanding the publishing industry so that you can better decide whether you are ready for the challenges—and rewards—and which steps to take first. So let's start by first analyzing the desired end result and pose some important questions that you need to research and answer.

Seven Significant Questions

1. Why am I writing this book? As with any business, your focus must be on targeting your market: know who will buy your book and why. Ask yourself, "What do I want the reader to learn from this book?"

2. What messages am I delivering that haven't been delivered before? A search on Amazon.com under the heading "leadership" lists 13,389 books, and 25,346 on "change". In Canada, ChaptersIndigo.com lists over 500 books in each category. Therefore, clearly define how your message differs from all the others and in what unique manner you will present it.

3. Where will I sell this book? Define whether you are going to use your book for back-of-the-room sales only, or whether you want it in retail stores across Canada. Will it be a text that appeals to an educational market? Know who will buy this book and where, and how you will market it to them. Many writers omit this vital step.

4. Which market am I writing for? Be clear on whether you are writing to a Canadian or US market. A misconception is to write for the US market in hope of larger sales. If you are an unknown Canadian speaker and author in North America, you are better to start with a Canadian focus to establish your reputation.

5. Will I self-publish or approach a publishing house? There is a huge difference between the two. As an author receiving royalties from a publishing house, your income is greatly diminished but your credibility is greatly enhanced. As a self-publisher, you are a micro-publishing house. Your product should match the quality of a reputable publisher. So now you are a book manufacturer, distributor, retailer and marketer.

6. Do I have the time to commit to this project? You need discipline, focus and time, not just for the writing, but also for production, continuous marketing, and administration. The book only lives on as long as you work at keeping it alive.

7. Do I have the finances to see this through from start to finish? If you self-publish, you need a generous budget to produce and market a quality product. Books published on a shoestring rarely experience optimal results or success. The information below will help you in making that decision.

Once you have answered these seven questions, you should have a better understanding of the type of book you want to produce—and why. As glamorous as it is to have a publisher accept your first book, chances are that your alternative will be self-publishing. Let's see why.

Traditional Publishing Houses

First, let's look at the odds. My literary agent once told me, "Of every 100 query letters an agent receives, he or she will pursue two of them. Of every 100 book proposals a publisher receives from agents, it will accept two of them." Putting it into context, when publishers look at book proposals, they need to answer:

- What's in it for us?
- Will the book make money and fill a niche?
- Who *is* this author?
- Does the author have sound credentials as an expert?
- Will this book interest the media?
- Will the author aggressively promote and market the book nationally?
- What similar books are competitors publishing?

Publishers rarely promote unknown authors. You have to be famous, and few of us are writing Harry Potter books. The credibility gained by being commercially published is a great bonus. It opens doors that were previously closed. My first book, *Business for Beginners*, which was self-published, is a large income generator. The second, *Big Ideas for Growing Your Small Business*, was published by McGraw-Hill Ryerson and has given me added national and international credibility, but far fewer monetary rewards.

The Publishing Process

Publishers rarely accept unsolicited manuscripts or query letters from authors. You need a literary agent to represent you, and there are few in Canada. An agent acts on your behalf, negotiates a contract in your favour, deals directly with the publishing house on most matters, and forwards your royalty cheques, less a commission and all expenses. The timeframe between submitting a query letter to getting published can take up to two years.

If a literary agent likes your one-page query letter, he or she will ask for a full proposal, including sample chapters. This is similar to preparing a business plan and takes thorough research and careful preparation. Read Elizabeth Lyon's *Non Fiction Book Proposals Anybody Can Write* (Blue Heron, 2002) to see the extent and format of a winning proposal.

You usually prepare all the manuscript and cover content, "about the author" information and the table of contents. You may also have to input editing corrections. You must supply detailed marketing information, and promise to promote the book as if you'd published it yourself. The average royalty is usually 10 percent of the retail price of books sold (less returns), and cheques are paid twice a year or quarterly, a few months after the close of each period. So unless you've written a *Who Moved My Cheese* bestseller, the income is minuscule compared to the work involved—but the feelings of satisfaction and achievement are wonderful.

So let's compare this to self-publishing.

Seven Strategies for Successful Self-Publishing

Self-publishing is a huge, long-term project. This chapter can only touch the surface; there are some wonderful books on the subject, including *How to Self Publish and Make Money*, by Nancy Wise and Marianne Crook (Sandhill Publishing/Crook, 1998). Marianne has written many books, and Nancy's company, Sandhill Book Marketing Inc., is a well-respected national distributor of self-published and small-press books. Their combined Canadian expertise is invaluable to a first-time author. Sandhill's web site is **www.sandhillbooks.com** .

Here are some of the important strategies you should follow if you choose this path.

1. Thoroughly research the market. Visit large bookstores, such as Chapters and Barnes & Noble, and surf the various online book sites. Study other books in your area of expertise to ensure you are not re-inventing the wheel. Your book must fill a *need* and a *niche*. If it is only of local interest and aimed at a limited market, how many copies do you realistically think you can sell?

2. Study the competition. Note what does and doesn't appeal to you in competitors' books. Look at style, presentation, layout, front and back covers, and what is missing from the content. Find out where your book can fill the gaps or cater to a niche market.

3. Study the art of non-fiction writing. *The Canadian Style* (Dundurn Press, 1997) and *Writing Creative Non-Fiction,* by Theodore Rees Cheney (Ten Speed Press, 2001), are two excellent reference books. Learn how to trim, edit and make each word carry a powerful message. Most people write far too much. Quantity is not necessarily quality. Study grammar, punctuation, and acceptable language usage. Attend writers' conferences or workshops. Writing is an art that takes time to learn, and you never stop learning. Nothing looks worse in a book than incorrect grammar and punctuation or typographical errors.

4. Work with a production team. You will need the services of an editor conversant with your subject, a text designer, cover designer, proofreader, and ideally, someone from the publishing industry who can analyze the book's technical details. You need their knowledge and experienced eyes to review the book in manuscript form as well as the final printer's proofs. They can often negotiate better pricing with printers and know which printer would be best for you.

5. Compare print-on-demand to commercial publishing. Your research may dictate that, to start, you require fewer books than a commercial print run. One of your publishing options for shorter runs is print-on-demand. Although financially more viable, there are some limitations, and the retail price of the book can be higher than its competitors. Because there are so many options offered in this area, research a reputable print-on-demand company such as Trafford Publishing. Their web site is **www.trafford.com** .

6. Be prepared to market, market, market! Your book won't sell unless you are prepared to promote it constantly. Sell sheets and press releases must be prepared, so learn how to write interesting press releases and media copy. Be prepared for book signings and free guest appearances, constant follow-up, and sending out up to 200 free review copies. That's just the start.

7. Talk to book distributors. Decide whether you want to handle retail sales yourself or use a distributor. You sell your book on a consignment basis to a distributor at 40 to 60 percent off retail price. Therefore, a book costing $3 to $5 to print should retail for approximately $22 to $25. You sell it to the distributor for $9 to $10, and you usually pay shipping costs. Distributors may pay you up to three months after each month's sales, and damaged books are returned to you.

The Ten-step Self-publishing Process

As a self-publisher, you are now in business as a manufacturer. Therefore your end product should be of top quality, as each page represents the quality of the information that you deliver verbally as a speaker. You are also in business to make money, so below are ten key areas that you should consider before you tackle this project.

1. Financing. The first step is a business plan for the book, including a cash flow projection and projections for income and expenses. Many of the costs incurred are mentioned below. As your first print run is usually more expensive due to initial production costs, the book per-unit cost will be significantly higher than for future reprints.

2. Text layout and design. Your book should be appealing to the eye, so hire a text designer and brainstorm. Once the final manuscript is edited, proofread and ready, the text designer lays the manuscript out in Quark or a similar publishing program. You may be given a choice of up to three layout designs and typefaces. Choose a traditional and readable font, such as Times New Roman 11-point. Small print discourages readers from continuing on.

3. Cover production. Books *are* judged by their titles and covers. A cover designer may give you up to three design choices, so be specific about your needs. Study other covers. What appeals to you? What makes them stand out on the shelves? Keep the cover simple yet effective. If you are cheap in your cover production, the book will probably look cheap. A well-designed two or three-colour cover can be most appealing to the eye.

4. Final proofing. Once the cover and text design are completed, a final proofreading by an expert proofreader is a must. The manuscript should be checked for technical details such as end-of-page hyphenations, typographical errors, header spacing, correct header levels, chapter names and page numbers, positioning and consistency, to name a few.

5. Printing. In my experience, a print run that allows for competitive pricing and a healthy profit for the self-publisher—including the distributor's percentage—is usually around 2,500 books. Some printers will also expect you to pay for overruns of up to 10 percent of the order. The first printing incurs some extra set-up charges. Your cost depends on paper and cover quality, the type of binding, and number of pages. You should allow at least twenty working days for a print run, plus time to proof the cover text and colours, and the printer's text proof. You may be expected to pay at least a one-third deposit and the balance on completion, so ask the printing company to clarify its terms of payment.

6. Finding customers. Although retail stores may be your main market, it is important to define secondary markets for your book. These are markets where you will make more money by selling larger quantities at a discounted price. Secondary markets may include your workshops or seminars, educational institutions, corporations or special interest groups.

7. Preparing for marketing. Contact people before the book is published to create excitement about its release. To effectively launch the book, be prepared to spend time marketing intensively, using a combination of the following:

- Preparing a one-page "sell sheet" (promotional flyer) for bookstores
- Obtaining book reviews in magazines and newspapers
- Sending press releases
- Offering to do book signings
- Offering to speak to special interest groups
- Sending out review and complimentary books with media kits

- Attending trade shows and conferences where the book gets exposure
- Preparing a brochure about yourself and your book
- Sending introductory e-mails and faxes to target markets
- Obtaining testimonials and permission to use them.

8. Distribution: Distributors don't usually accept a book until it is published and they have assessed its sales potential. Unfortunately, you then miss out on the "new release" publicity window in their catalogues and from their sales representatives. It is industry etiquette to use only one distributor. Most retail bookstores, particularly chains such as Chapters, will not open an account with a single-title author unless you are a local author or the book is selling like hot tamales. Without a distributor, you will spend your whole day, every day, working on selling your book.

9. Shipping and inventory control. Possibly the best shipping method is to open an account with Canada Post's small business bulk mailing service, which includes Express, Expedited or Regular services. You will need a selection of custom-sized boxes for shipping small quantities, padded mailer bags for review or single copies, bubble wrap or foam chips, strong packaging tape, address labels and marking pens.

Books should be carefully stored at no more than 40 percent humidity and 21 degrees Celsius, or 70 degrees Fahrenheit. Although temperatures can exceed this mark without harming the books, excessive humidity damages them. In damp climates, invest in a dehumidifier, a heater and a humidity/temperature gauge (total cost approximately $500).

Depending on your print run and page count, you may need room to house your books. For example, 2,500 six-by-nine-inch books (300 pages each), plus overruns, pack into sixty-four cases weighing fifty pounds a case. That's 3,200 pounds of books. I found that weight-lifting helped to build my muscles so I could heave the cases without doing myself physical damage.

10. Legal and copyright requirements.

a. *Copyright:* Although under Canadian law copyright is automatic on publication, for maximum protection you should apply to register copyright on your book as soon you know the publication date. The current fee is $65. Contact the Canadian Intellectual Property Office, web site: **www.cipo.gc.ca** .

b. *Books in Print:* If your book is to be distributed in the US, advance book information should be completed so that your book gets into the US retail book system. If you self-publish using print-on-demand, clarify with the POD publisher whether your book is eligible. Contact R.R. Bowker Data Collection Center, web site: **www.bowker.com** .

c. *ISBN and CIP:* Give yourself plenty of time to get both your ISBN (International Standard Book Number) and CIP (Cataloguing in Publication classification). You need both before publication. Be sure your book includes the ISBN as a bar code on the back cover. Otherwise, bookstores may not sell it because it doesn't scan by computer. It is your responsibility to purchase the bar code, which can be obtained through label companies. Contact the National Library of Canada, web site: **www.nlc-bnc.ca** .

d. *Legal Deposit:* After your book is published, you must send two copies to the National Library of Canada as a legal deposit. Ask for these forms with your ISBN information, or you can get forms online at **www.nlc_bnc.ca/6/25/s25-201-e.html** .

e. *Access Copyright:* Once your book is published, contact Access Copyright (the Canadian copyright licensing agency) for a membership agreement. Membership is no charge, and you will be reimbursed each year for the use of your book by agencies and institutions that photocopy portions of it. Access Copyright's web site: **www.accesscopyright.ca** .

Which Path to Follow?

Each author's publishing needs are unique, so talk to as many people as you can who have been successfully published and who have successfully self-published. The more research you do the better equipped you will be to make the right decision. There is nothing more satisfying than seeing a book with your name on the cover, unless it's seeing people flock to buy it. If you have a great idea for a book and a dream to publish, make it a reality. Just remember; it is also a business, so don't forget to make it a profitable venture.

Frances McGuckin
21944 6th Ave.
Langley, BC V2Z 1R6
T: 604-530-3601
Toll free: 888-771-2771
F: 604-530-6447
contact@smallbizpro.com
www.smallbizpro.com

About Frances McGuckin

Frances McGuckin, the **Small Biz Pro**, is an award-winning management consultant, columnist, professional speaker and best-selling author in the field of small business. She has been nominated for many awards, including the 1999 Canadian Entrepreneur of the Year. She was named one of Vancouver's Five Most Influential Women in Business in 2002, and was awarded Langley's Business Person of the Year in 1999.

Frances' self-published book, *Business for Beginners*, has sold over 125,000 copies. The third edition was released in January 2003. Electronic rights have been purchased by Intuit Canada, and a Russian version is to be published in 2003. The book is used throughout Canada and the United States for many self-employment programs and courses at colleges and community business development offices. McGraw Hill-Ryerson released the sequel, *Big Ideas for Growing Your Small Business*, in December of 2000 as part of its SOHO series, which features top Canadian business writers. Frances is also a business columnist for a variety of publications and e-zines in both Canada and the United States.

Drawing on a wealth of business knowledge amassed over thirty years, Frances has taught entrepreneurship skills for eighteen years. Her home-based businesses, **Eastleigh Publications**, **Eastleigh Management Services** and **SmallBizPro.com Services**, are in their twentieth year. She is a popular national media guest, involved in many community activities, and teaches the first accredited Equine Entrepreneurship course in British Columbia at Kwantlen University College in Langley.

A dynamic and inspiring speaker who travels extensively throughout Canada and the United States teaching entrepreneurship and delivering motivational keynotes, Frances' mission in life is to stop small business failure. Her customized, energized and interactive keynotes and seminars motivate both people—and businesses—to take action to realize their dreams. She speaks to a variety of audiences, including corporations, meeting planners, national associations, women, youth, entrepreneurs, speakers and writers, to name a few. She is a Professional member of the Canadian Association of Professional Speakers (CAPS), and treasurer for the Vancouver chapter.

Mind, Body and Spirit: Change Your Mind, Change Your Life

by Lynn Robinson

You may find at some point that you wonder how you fit in. Or you may question what you have to offer. Why would anyone want to hear what you have to say? It's all been said before. There's nothing special about you. And yet something inside you knows that you're meant to be out there speaking, sharing your message.

You're not alone. Every speaker goes through this at some point and perhaps even more than once. There may be times when you question yourself and you're not even sure what your message really is. But something keeps you going, that inner drive that can't logically be explained. That's when you know you're hooked and there's no going back.

A driving inner passion and desire is the only thing that will keep you going when you experience challenges. Without that, you'll give up. With it, you won't be able to.

As much as you need strategies for your business, you also need to have strategies in place to take care of yourself. You are the business. You make the information come alive. Speaking is one of the most rewarding professions you can be in, and one that can be the most personally challenging. Because of this, self-care and self-management are crucial to your success.

No matter what just happened in your life, when you step up to the podium you have to be on. You're there to inspire, motivate, educate, and make a difference in your audiences' lives. It can be a scary place and the most fulfilling place to be. You need to be able to deliver in the highs and the lows no matter what. To be able to deliver, balance is crucial.

This chapter is written with the assumption that you are an expert on your material. This information is meant to overlay and enhance your experience and the experience of your audience.

Your Mind

Your mind is an amazingly powerful tool. Every thought you have affects your results and your future. As a speaker, you want to be able to harness your mind power so that you're able to handle whatever comes your way.

Have you ever wondered why some people have major challenges and still follow through with professionalism and grace while others aren't able to handle the smallest change in plans without an inappropriate response? Or why, no matter what the economic climate, one person flourishes while someone else goes out of business? It's not what you experience but rather your attitude towards it that determines your results, and your attitude is determined by your state of mind. By changing your mind, you change your results.

All learning, behaviour and change take place unconsciously, which means they happen automatically and outside your awareness. That's why, without thinking, you continue to do the things you know aren't getting you the results you want. It's programmed in. The good news is that it isn't hardwired in and you can change the program. Here are some simple techniques that can help you change these programs easily and quickly.

1. Self-talk: affirmations. One of the ways you program your results is by self-talk. What are you saying to yourself most of the time? Are you telling yourself what you want to achieve and how competent you are, or the exact opposite? Positive affirmations can change your state of mind. Negative affirmations can also change your state of mind. The only difference is that one moves you closer to what you want and the other moves you closer to what you don't want. Begin to notice what you say to yourself and start programming in what you want.

2. Dealing with anxiety. At some point, whether you're just starting out or a seasoned speaker, you will be offered an opportunity that stretches you. You may even find that thinking about it gives you a feeling of anxiety. You know you'll be able to pull it off and do a great job and yet you still have that anxious feeling. Here's a simple way to overcome that feeling and totally change your experience.

Take a moment to think about the event. It's best to close your eyes so you remove any external stimulation and can focus all your attention on this process. Imagine you're now fifteen minutes past the *successful* completion of the event. What do you see? What do you hear? What are you doing? What are you saying to yourself and how does it feel to have successfully completed the event? Notice the word "successful" is key.

Did you know that when you feel anxious, you're also following this process? The only difference is that you're imagining what it will be like if you're unsuccessful. It's impossible for you to feel anxious if you are focused on the success of the event.

Try this. You'll love the results. It makes anxiety-creating events much more fun for you. Remember that if the event hasn't happened yet, you're just making it up. It's all in your mind. My philosophy is that if you're going to make it up, make up something great. Use your mind to empower yourself.

3. Mental Rehearsal. I've had the opportunity and privilege of working with athletes in the past, coaching them on their mental performance. What I realized is that speakers and trainers need many of the same mental skills. To perform at your best you not only have to be skilled in your area of expertise, but also mentally and emotionally.

Mental rehearsal is one of the most useful techniques you can practice to perfect your performance. Studies have shown the effectiveness of mental rehearsal. Just think about how successful Tiger Woods has been. This, by the way, does not eliminate the need for actual practice!

Run through your event exactly as you want it to be. See yourself doing it perfectly. Rehearse it over and over so that by the time you actually do it, it will be as if you've done it many times before.

It's a great way to be prepared for any problems that might arise, such as your mike not working, or your remote not working. You can run through some "what ifs" and come up with the solutions just in case.

4. Changing your state. As a speaker, one of the most important skills you'll master is control of your mental and emotional state. You'll want to have the flexibility to access a full range of emotions because the only way to lead your audience to where you want them to go is to go there first. One technique you can use to access a positive state is called anchoring. Once you've completed the process once, you can access it at any time.

Decide how you want to feel—for example, confident. Imagine a circle on the floor in front of you. Give it a colour. While standing outside the circle, think about a time in your past, a specific time, when you felt totally confident. It can be in any context, perhaps in sports or during a sale. As you think about that time, think about it as if you're experiencing the feeling now. Let the feeling of confidence flow through your body. Feel it building, stronger and stronger. When you feel it intensely throughout your body, step into your circle and bring the confidence into the circle with you. Stand there for a moment, then back out of the circle, leaving the confidence in the circle. Repeat the process three or four times. This is now your power circle. Think of a speaking event in the future, and as you think about it step into your power circle and feel the feeling of confidence as you think about the event. You've now linked the feeling of confidence with the event.

You can also imagine the circle on the floor at the edge of the stage, and as you step onto the stage, notice that feeling of confidence flowing through you.

Your Emotional Wellbeing

Your emotions play an important role in your performance and success. Your technical skills may land you the job, but maintaining a long term relationship will be influenced by your emotional maturity.

Begin to notice your response to people and situations. For example, if you find your response is often anger, frustration or resentment, these emotions can limit you and have the potential to erupt at the most inappropriate times.

Ninety-three percent of your communication is non-verbal, which means everyone is picking up a lot more information about you than you might like.

Emotions like anger, frustration and resentment are just an indication that something isn't right. The sooner you take care of what's not working, the sooner the emotions will dissipate. By ignoring these indicators, you run the risk of having them surface at an inappropriate time in the form of an inappropriate response to someone in your audience, a meeting planner, a client or even a colleague. It can be uncomfortable when your "stuff" shows up. And you can be sure it will.

When emotions surface, notice them and just ask yourself what this is really about. It's very rarely about whatever is happening at that moment. It's more likely to be a build-up of unresolved emotions and issues from the past. It's impossible for someone to trigger an emotional response from you unless it's there lurking somewhere inside you. Because speakers spend most of their time in front of people, you want to make sure you've taken care of any emotional hot buttons you're aware of. Holding on to them puts you in a very vulnerable position.

Invest in yourself and find a professional who can help you release and deal with your unresolved emotions.

Your Body

As a speaker, you spend much of your time on the road, going from airport to airport, hotel to hotel. This can be very grueling on the body. The body is often the last thing we pay attention to and somehow it just keeps going. We think.

To stay balanced and to maintain your energy level throughout your speaking engagements, you'll want to consciously incorporate some simple daily practices into your routine. These will help you perform professionally at all times.

The mind–body connection means that everything you do for your body directly affects your mind. Conversely, everything you do for your mental state directly affects your body. Although I've separated the two for the purposes of learning, there truly is no separation.

Your Body Needs Nourishment

When you're traveling, it's a good idea to keep something with you to snack on in case you don't have time to sit down to a proper meal. A bag of almonds, a piece of fruit or an energy bar are good choices.

By feeding your body, which includes your brain, you can stay energized and alert. This will save you time in the long run because your body needs fuel to perform optimally.

Your Body Needs Exercise

If you have the option, book a hotel with a gym or pool. You don't need to do a full workout, just something to keep your body moving and get the blood circulating. Exercise also stimulates the neural networks in the brain and gets them moving. You might even find ideas popping into your head while you're focusing on your body.

If there is no gym or you're not a gym person, get some fresh air. Take a walk. One of the biggest obstacles to doing this is feeling that you need a lot of time for it. Not so. Fifteen minutes is better than not walking. Sometimes you get your best insights or even stories for your presentation while you're walking. Stretching will also limber you up and get things moving.

Your Body Needs Relaxation

By taking just five minutes to relax, you'll reap immediate benefits. Relaxation lowers blood pressure, heart rate, and respiratory response while improving circulation, to name a few benefits.

If you're a high-energy person, you might think that by relaxing you'll lose your momentum. On the contrary! This is just another way to replenish your body's resources and re-energize yourself. There is only one catch. There are side effects. You may find that you are more focused, creative, and alert!

You can use a number of techniques to relax. I'll list a few to get you started. And remember, relaxing is a learned skill, which means it gets easier with practice.

1. Breathing exercises. One of the fastest ways to relax your body is to focus on your breathing and breathe into your lower abdomen rather than your upper chest. Breathe in slowly to the count of four, hold for two counts and breathe out slowly to the count of four. This is a calming breathing technique and can be used at any time throughout the day, whenever you notice your stress level rising. This can be done anywhere at any time, unnoticed by anyone else. There is no need to exaggerate your breathing. Just breathe naturally.

2. Meditation. There are many different ways to meditate, depending on your purpose. You may want to be more relaxed; you may want to get focused, gain clarity and insight; or simply to start your day centred and balanced.

You may be someone who has resisted meditation or tried it and given up because you thought you had to still your mind and have no thoughts to be able to meditate. That is an unrealistic expectation in Western culture. You'd be surprised how many people meditate to relax and maintain balance in their busy lives.

Meditation can take many forms. Always begin by finding a comfortable place where you won't be disturbed, close your eyes to eliminate visual distractions, and take a moment to do the breathing exercise mentioned above to relax. Go into meditation with a purpose: to relax, to get insight on a problem, or perhaps to receive guidance. Hold the purpose in your mind and allow the answers to come.

This may sound strange to you, but from a scientific perspective, by slowing down the frequency of your brain waves (which you do when you relax or meditate) you access different parts and functions of your brain. As an example, the alpha state accesses creativity and relaxation while theta accesses inspiration.

Something you can also do is think of a colour and focus your attention on the colour. As your mind wanders, just bring your attention back to the colour. Do this for at least five minutes, but preferably for fifteen to twenty minutes. This will revitalize you and help you focus. You may even find that at times you get flashes of inspiration as you sit quietly.

This is great to do on an airplane. People just think you're sleeping. You can also use meditation to give yourself a focused start to the day or to get centred before a presentation.

3. Guided visualization CDs. If you find you have a very busy mind and it's not easy for you to sit quietly to refresh your body, there are some CDs designed to guide you into a relaxed state. When I first began meditation, I found the CDs very useful. This is a great way to condition your body to learn to relax.

Your Spirit

It's your spirit that will inspire, motivate, and influence others—the essence of who you truly are. There are many people who are out there doing the same thing you're doing, and the only thing that makes you unique and different is you. It's the ability to be yourself in front of your audience. To make a connection with your audience you need to be fully aligned in body, mind and spirit. When you're aligned, you can connect at the level that makes a difference in people's lives.

In order for your true spirit to emerge, there must be congruence between what you're doing and who you are. It takes believing in yourself. If the congruence isn't there, your audience will see right through you. Do you believe in what you speak about? Are you living what you speak? Do you have the same principles and values on the platform as you do off it? Do you model what you say? This doesn't mean you have to be perfect. It just means you're doing the best you can to practice what you present. Remember, we're all human. As much as you're there to inspire, motivate, and educate your audience, you're also there to learn. I believe it's true that we teach what we need to learn.

Your spirit moves you from your head to your heart. It's what drives your passion. Your spirit connects you to the purpose that encompasses something greater than you. Your purpose takes you outside of yourself and answers the questions, "Who else do I want to affect? What will this do for others? What kind of a difference will I make?" The answer to these questions will be your guiding force.

Once you're in front of your audience, it's time to let go and trust. You know you've done everything you can do to prepare yourself, you have a clear motivation for what you're doing, and you're committed to make this the best experience for everyone, including yourself.

Here is a set of principles I'd like to share with you that will empower you and support you in your career.

Principles of an Excellent Speaker

1. My focus is on my audience. It's about them, not about me.
2. I have all the resources I need to be an excellent speaker.
3. There is no failure, only feedback.
4. I am in control of my mind and therefore of my results.
5. I am totally present and willing to give 100 percent.
6. I am willing to do what it takes to make a difference in people's lives.
7. I give to myself first so I have something to give to others.

I'm not suggesting these are necessarily always true, but if you act as if they are you'll be amazed at your results.

Putting It Together

Most speakers and trainers don't take the time to take care of mind, body and spirit. There never seems to be enough time because something else is always the priority. What you'll learn, as we all have, is that if you ignore your own needs, eventually something will suffer. It may be your health, your performance level, or your relationships with your friends and family, but without balance between mind, body and spirit in your life, something's got to give.

I'm writing the last of this chapter at our cabin in the forest, sitting on the deck in the beautiful sunshine. The ocean is a few feet away and I can hear the waves lapping against the rocks. I almost didn't come because of my busy schedule and as I sit here I'm reminded of how important it is to nurture your soul. This is what life is all about; this is what allows you to have something to give.

Remember to take time to nurture your mind, body and spirit because the world is waiting to hear what you have to say.

Lynn Robinson
The Robinson Group Training &
  Consulting Corp.
928 Kent St.
White Rock, BC V4B 4T1
P: 604-542-3008
F: 604-542-0889
lynn@therobinsongroup.ca
www.therobinsongroup.ca

About Lynn Robinson

Lynn is an international keynote speaker, trainer and coach working with companies in Canada, the USA and the UK. As a Certified Trainer in Neuro-linguistic Programming (NLP) and Hypnotherapy, Lynn brings an added dimension—the science of the mind—to interpersonal communication skills. She has been named the "Top NLP Speaker in British Columbia". Her enthusiasm and passion for life leaves clients feeling refreshed, inspired and uplifted.

Lynn's audio CDs tap the power of the mind to find balance, sharpen focus and assist learning. She is also the author of *The Magical Mind*, to be released in 2004. Her book, CDs and presentations cover the following key areas:

- It's all in your head—How your thoughts create your results

- Self-limitations—Unleash your true potential

- Power of the mind—How it affects your performance
- Filtering your experience—What are you missing?
- Programming yourself for success—It's an inside job
- Brain waves—More than just a good idea
- Influencing language—Speaking consciously

Lynn shares these practical tools with her clients to help them develop effective interpersonal communication skills, build co-operative relationships, and increase performance results. Her purpose is to help people recognize their personal power and realize they have it within themselves to change.

As a trainer, Lynn works with corporations, developing and facilitating programs that apply accelerated learning techniques to increase retention and integration of communication skills. Lynn also presents courses for NLP Practitioner certification, NLP Master Practitioner certification, NLP Coaching certification, leadership, advanced sales training, executive team development, corporate visioning and "train the trainer".

As a coach with more than twenty years' experience Lynn has developed programs that break through your personal limitations and propel you towards clarity, self-motivation and success.

People leave Lynn's sessions with fresh perspectives, new ideas, and practical skills that help them to be more effective.

Lynn is in the process of completing her PhD in hypnotherapy to further develop her expertise in the power of the mind and how it affects performance in business. She is a member of the American Board of Neuro-linguistic Programming, the Canadian Association of Neuro-linguistic Programming and the American Board of Hypnotherapy. She is also on the board of directors of CAPS and the Tri-Cities Hospice, and was a founding faculty member of Waters Corporate University.

Index of Contributors

Contributors are listed in the order they appear.

Elaine Allison
Positive Presentations Plus Inc.
2241 Stafford Ave.
Port Coquitlam, BC V3C 4X5
P: 604-723-7774
F: 604-944-7186
eallison@presentationsplusinc.com
www.presentationsplusinc.com

- Business management
- Entrepreneurship
- Marketing, sales and service
- Conflict management in the workplace
- E-commerce and e-business

Lorne Kelton
ThinkShift Technologies Inc.
9133 Evancio Cres.
Richmond, BC V7E 5J2
P: 604-277-9911
F: 604-304-0141
lorne@thinkshift.com
www.thinkshift.com

- Motivation
- Training
- Time/self management
- Writing
- Sales
- Communication

Sherrin Western
SHERVIN Communications Inc.
Ste 101, 8557 Government Rd.
Burnaby, BC V3N 4S9
P: 604-422-0174
F: 604-422-0175
sherrin@goshervin.com
www.goshervin.com

- Maximize Your Brand in the Marketplace
- Customers Really are Everything!
- Building Business Relationships for Prosperity
- Marketing Your Business is Not Optional!

Natalie Forstbauer
Dr. Feel Good
P: 604-737-3632
F: 760-462-2910
natalie@dare2feel.com
www.dare2feel.com

- Healthy Living and Life Balance
- Corporate Health
- Entrepreneurship
- E-Commerce and E-Business
- Women In Business

Margaret F. Hope, M.Ed.
Lionsgate Training Ltd.
4649 Hastings St.
Burnaby, BC V5C 2K6

P: 604-320-7613
F: 604-320-1660
mhope@lionsgatetraining.com
www.lionsgatetraining.com
- You're Speaking—But Are You Connecting? (Speeches, Presentations)
- Self-Promotion 101 (Networking, Marketing Yourself)
- Persuading and Influencing
- Creativity
- Business Etiquette

Abegael Fisher-Lang
Mythopoetica Storytelling
Box 16206, Lynn Valley PO
North Vancouver, BC V7J 3S9
P: 604-985-5168
afl@mythopoetica.ca
www.mythopoetica.ca
- Storytelling

David Granirer, MA, RPC
Psychocomic.com Presentations Inc.
3633 Triumph St.
Vancouver, BC V5K 1V4
P: 604-205-9242
F: 604-205-9243
david@psychocomic.com
www.psychocomic.com
- Humour in the Workplace
- Using Humour to Beat Stress
- Leading with Laughter
- How to Captivate Your Audience with Stand-Up Comedy
- Humour and Diversity Training

Carla Rieger
YES Education Systems
Ste 138, 2906 West Broadway
Vancouver, BC V6K 2G8
P: 604-267-2381
F: 604-222-2267
info@yeseducationsystems.com
www.yeseducationsystems.com
- Managing Change with a Sense of Humour
- Creative Resolutions: Finding Win-Win Agreements in a Diverse Workplace
- Team Play: Bringing a Sense of Fun-loving Community to Your Work Group
- Get Your Grouch Potato Off the Sofa: A Lighthearted Approach to Dealing with Difficult Behaviours
- Innovative Strategic Planning: An Enjoyable Way to Build Group Consensus & Create Effective Action Plans

Geoffrey X. Lane
Lane Consulting Group Inc.
Ste. 566, 916 West Broadway
Vancouver, BC V5Z 1K7
P: 604-877-0089
F: 604-877-0029
geoffrey@geoffreyxlane.com
www.geoffreyxlane.com
- Motivation
- Communication and Public Speaking as Tools for Leaders
- Leadership
- Personal Effectiveness

Cheryl Cran
Synthesis At Work
Ste. 1000, 355 Burrard St.
Vancouver, BC V6C 2G8

P: 604-552-9640
Toll free: 877-900-5010
F: 604-552-8588
info@cherylcran.com
www.cherylcran.com

- Say What You Mean, Get the Results You Want

- Powerful Beyond Measure: Empowered to Succeed

- We're Changing as Fast as We Can!

- Customers Want What They Want and They Want It Now

- Why Can't Everyone Get Along? Teamwork solutions

- Leadership at the Speed of Change: Flexible Leadership

David Gouthro
The Consulting Edge: Movers & Shakers, Inc.
23-1551 Johnston St.
Vancouver, BC V6H 3R9
P: 604-685-6858
Toll free: 800-685-6818
F: 604-685-6242
dgouthro@theconsultingedge.com
www.theconsultingedge.com

- Building individual and organizational courage

- Leadership development

- Team development

- Creativity and creative problem solving

- Effective thinking with Smartskills™ and One Smart World™

- Emotional intelligence

- Strategic planning

Linda Edgecombe
Learning Edge Resources Corporation
2102 Bowron St.
Kelowna, BC V1V 2L6
P: 250-868-9601
F: 250-868-9740
www.lindaedgecombe.com
info@lindaedgecombe.com

- Career/Lifestyle
- Health/Wellness
- Humour
- Leadership
- Motivation
- Stress

Frances McGuckin
21944 6th Ave.
Langley, BC V2Z 1R6
T: 604-530-3601
Toll free: 888-771-2771
F: 604-530-6447
contact@smallbizpro.com
www.smallbizpro.com

- Business growth
- Low-cost marketing
- Entrepreneurship
- Managing business change positively
- Organization
- Financial control
- Goal setting and balance

Lynn Robinson
The Robinson Group Training & Consulting Corp.
928 Kent St.
White Rock, BC V4B 4T1
P: 604-542-3008
F: 604-542-0889
lynn@therobinsongroup.ca
www.therobinsongroup.ca

- It's all in your head: how your thoughts create your results
- Self-limitations: unleash your true potential
- Power of the mind: how it affects your performance
- Filtering your experience: what are you missing?
- Programming yourself for success: it's an inside job
- Brain waves: more than just a good idea
- Influencing language: speaking consciously

ISBN 141200927-8

9 781412 009270